www.wadsworth.com

www.wadsworth.com is the World Wide Web site for Thomson Wadsworth and is your direct source to dozens of online resources.

At *www.wadsworth.com* you can find out about supplements, demonstration software, and student resources. You can also send email to many of our authors and preview new publications and exciting new technologies.

www.wadsworth.com
Changing the way the world learns®

Current Perspectives
Readings from InfoTrac® College Edition

Cultural Anthropology
and Globalization

THOMSON
™
WADSWORTH

Australia • Canada • Mexico • Singapore • Spain
United Kingdom • United States

THOMSON
™
WADSWORTH

Current Perspectives: Readings from InfoTrac® College Edition
Cultural Anthropology and Globalization

Publisher: *Eve Howard*
Senior Acquisitions Editor: *Lin Marshall*
Assistant Editor: *Nicole Root*
Editorial Assistant: *Kelly McMahon*
Technology Project Manager: *Dee Dee Zobian*
Senior Marketing Manager: *Wendy Gordon*
Marketing Assistant: *Annabelle Yang*
Senior Marketing Communications
    Manager: *Linda Yip*
Project Manager, Editorial Production:
    Brenda Ginty

Creative Director: *Robert Hugel*
Print Buyer: *Karen Hunt*
Production Service: *Rozi Harris, Interactive*
    Composition Corporation
Permissions Editor: *Joohee Lee*
Cover Designer: *Larry Didona*
Cover Image: *Photolibrary.com/Photonica*
Cover and Text Printer: *Thomson West*
Compositor: *Interactive Composition Corporation*

Printed in the United States of America
1 2 3 4 5 6 7 09 08 07 06 05

For more information about our products,
contact us at:
Thomson Learning Academic Resource Center
1-800-423-0563

For permission to use material from this text
or product, submit a request online at
http://www.thomsonrights.com.
Any additional questions about permissions
can be submitted by email to
thomsonrights@thomson.com.

Library of Congress Control Number:
2004116853

ISBN 0-495-00810-9

Thomson Higher Education
10 Davis Drive
Belmont, CA 94002-3098
USA

Asia (including India)
Thomson Learning
5 Shenton Way
#01-01 UIC Building
Singapore 068808

Australia/New Zealand
Thomson Learning Australia
102 Dodds Street
Southbank, Victoria 3006
Australia

Canada
Thomson Nelson
1120 Birchmount Road
Toronto, Ontario M1K 5G4
Canada

UK/Europe/Middle East/Africa
Thomson Learning
High Holborn House
50-51 Bedford Row
London WC1R 4LR
United Kingdom

Latin America
Thomson Learning
Seneca, 53
Colonia Polanco
11560 Mexico
D.F. Mexico

Spain (including Portugal)
Thomson Paraninfo
Calle Magallanes, 25
28015 Madrid, Spain

Contents

Preface

"It has been said that arguing against globalization is like arguing against the laws of gravity."
—Kofi Annan, Secretary-General of the United Nations and 2001 Nobel Peace Prize recipient

The term *globalization* has quickly become one of the most widely used buzzwords of contemporary political and academic debate. Outsourcing by corporations based in the United States and Europe is resulting in unprecedented transfers of capital, technology, and jobs, most recently to China and India. And conversely, people in Tennessee and South Carolina are getting all sorts of high-paying jobs as Nissan and BMW build auto plants in those states. Moreover, U.S. corporations are profiting handsomely by using, quite happily, low-paid laborers from Mexico. Directly or indirectly, globalization is producing social, cultural, political, and economic consequences that are remolding the lives of all the world's peoples. The great debate on globalization is in full swing; some see it as a battle between winners and losers, while others see it not as a debate, but an ongoing quest to find the best uses of increased interconnectedness of our ever-evolving global society.

The purpose of this reader is to elicit lively classroom discussions about the real-world challenges and opportunities that we face as we move toward a more global community. *Current Perspectives: Readings from InfoTrac College Edition: Cultural Anthropology and Globalization* is designed for use in the introductory cultural anthropology course; however, it also can be used in various disciplines—sociology, political science, economics, and business (to name a few)—in which the impact and effect of globalization are examined. The collection of articles was chosen from various periodicals to provide a wide range of discussion materials that can be used to supplement any introductory cultural anthropology curriculum in which the issue of globalization is addressed.

InfoTrac College Edition is an online research and learning center with over 10 million full-text articles from nearly 5,000 scholarly and popular periodicals (including *The New York Times*). These articles are updated daily and date back to 1980. This fully searchable library is available from any computer with Internet access. In addition, *InfoTrac* includes *InfoWrite,* a tool that aids in the development of research writing skills by offering tips on choosing topics, crediting sources, developing thesis statements, enhancing grammar and word usage, using quotations, composing introductions and conclusions, and creating drafts and revisions. In addition, *InfoTrac* now has a Critical Thinking resource center. That is, it provides instructions about how to determine whether or not a particular argument ought to be believed. This includes distinguishing facts from opinions and primary sources from secondary sources, evaluating information, and recognizing deceptive arguments and stereotypes.

In addition to providing students and instructors with recent articles to utilize in a classroom setting, this reader gives students and instructors the tools to begin their own original research. Using *InfoTrac College Edition's* new *InfoMark* capabilities, students and instructors can create their own *InfoTrac* Virtual Readers. With minimal effort, this resource allows you to search, compile, and create a list of articles that can be formatted into an electronic reader. Detailed instructions on how to use this new resource can be found at the back of this reader or at http://www.infotrac-college.com.

We invite you to use *Current Perspectives: Readings from InfoTrac College Edition: Cultural Anthropology and Globalization* as a tool to complement and expand classroom discussion in your introductory cultural anthropology course. We hope that the combination of your cultural anthropology textbook, the tools available in *InfoTrac College Edition,* and this reader will enrich the classroom experience for both the student and instructor.

To ensure that this collection of articles meets your needs as both students and instructors, I encourage you to send me your thoughts on how we can improve upon this volume. Please send your comments to me at nicole.root@thomson.com.

Nicole Root
Assistant Editor, Anthropology
Thomson Higher Education

1

Tempest in a Coffeepot: Starbucks Invades the World

Jackson Kuhl

Reaction to globalization of Starbucks coffeehouses

The Seventh International Festival of Arts and Ideas, held last June in New Haven, Connecticut, was one of those upscale boho fairs filled with puppets and Andean pan pipes aimed at the Birkenstock-and-Volvo set. A guest speaker was explaining why foreigners hate us. He railed against the "homogenization" of global culture and the threat of "monoculture"— that is, the worldwide replacement of individual, indigenous stores and restaurants with international chains.

"Monoculture," according to the speaker, is why they—Europeans, Arabs, everybody—despise us: They're under cultural siege. Starbucks, he warned, had just opened its first store in Zurich, the alleged birthplace of European coffee, and the Seattle-based chain would do everything it could to displace every native coffee shop in the city. Like infesting alien pods, American culture threatens to transmogrify the planet, as the speaker put it, into one big New Jersey. Starbucks was just one example.

The speaker was Benjamin R. Barber, professor of civil society at the University of Maryland, professional anti-capitalist, and relentless self-promoter.

Reason, Jan 2003, v34, i8, p55(3).

(You can tour his glossy temple of ego at benjaminbarber.com.) My reaction to his scenario was simple: If the Swiss don't like Starbucks, they shouldn't patronize Starbucks. To Barber this is fatuous; he is a proponent of "strong democracy," under which a bureaucracy would restrain Starbucks to protect mom-and-pop coffeehouses.

I suspect there is room in Zurich for both. The Swiss like their coffee so much that a whole institution, the Johann Jacobs Museum, is dedicated to the subject. (The price of admission includes a free cup in its dining room.) What is even more thought provoking than the new Starbucks in Zurich is the chain's expansion into Arab countries, whose people have a much longer connection to the coffee bean.

Coffee's history is worth pausing over, because its complex international development raises the question of whether Barber and like-minded critics know what they're whining about. Coffea arabica originated in the Ethiopian highlands, where the raw, unroasted beans were masticated and the leaves brewed like tea by the locals. How it spread down to the coast and across the Red Sea to Arabia is uncertain, but it is in al-Makkha that, according to popular belief, a cup of coffee was first brewed around 1200 A.D. Soon coffee made al-Makkha fabulously wealthy. Its plantations were guarded by armies, and fortresses served as bean storehouses. Four centuries later, merchants from Egypt to India lined the docks of al-Makkha, the city from which we derive the word mocha, clamoring for the stuff.

A member of the Sufi order of Shadhili mystics is credited with first brewing coffee, or qahwa (short for qahwa al-bon, "wine of the bean" in Arabic), and it quickly spread through the group: Members used it to sustain their all-night spinning ceremonies. These "whirling dervishes," as the West called them, attempted to alter their consciousness through ecstatic gyration, and thus get closer to God. Caffeine helped them do it. Pretty soon, the wandering Shadhilis had transported coffee throughout the Islamic world, where it shed its religious trappings and became an everyday drink enjoyed by commoner and royal alike.

Not that every ruler endorsed it. In 1511 coffee was banned in Mecca as being too similar to alcohol. (The ban was overturned 14 years later.) A century later, the Turkish sultan Murad IV became alarmed that coffeehouses were centers of political criticism, so he enacted the 1633 version of campaign finance reform: Coffee was banned, cafes destroyed, and drinkers beaten or beheaded. In 1675 England's King Charles II ordered closings for the same reasons, but the public outcry was such that he revoked the ban two days before it was to go into effect.

The former coffeehouse owners of the Ottoman world relocated to the more hospitable climate of Europe. Merchant trade, European travelers, and Turkish diplomats also spread the bean west. But coffee didn't enter the Continental mainstream until after the Ottoman Turks were routed from their siege of Vienna by the Poles in 1683, when they left 500 bags of coffee beans behind (the sultan's ban presumably having been reversed). Vienna's first coffeehouse opened two years later. As the result of a single battle, Ottoman expansion was halted and European cafe culture was born—making Vienna, not Zurich, the birthplace of European coffee.

Americans consumed a little over 10 pounds of coffee per capita in 2000, with 52 percent over age 18 saying they drank coffee the day before, according to a survey by the National Coffee Association of USA. But compared to either the Viennese or Barber's beloved Swiss, we're teetotalers. Austrians drink about 14 pounds, the Swiss 15.5. There are over 4,500 Starbucks outlets in the U.S., or one store for every 61,000 people. In Austria, which boasts but five Starbucks outlets, the ratio is one for every 608,000; in Switzerland (12 stores) it's one for every 1.6 million. There's more of a market for coffee in those two countries but fewer Starbucks per capita. Where's the hegemony Barber warns about?

Perhaps Starbucks hasn't had time yet. The chain has been expanding in the Middle East for years, with 80 stores in Arab countries such as Bahrain, Kuwait, and Saudi Arabia. Nearby countries such as Egypt and Syria have none. The absence may be explained by a notable lack of interest in coffee: The average Egyptian consumes only 0.13 pound in a year; the average Syrian, two pounds. Obviously Starbucks goes where there's a taste for joe. The three Arab nations with the lowest Starbucks-to-people ratios are the United Arab Emirates (UAE) (one per 104,000), Kuwait (one per 111,000), and Qatar (one per 267,000). Yet the Lebanese have 11 stores, one for every 336,000 people, and consume 9.5 pounds of coffee per capita, putting them on a par with Americans and outstripping the other three: The UAE consumes five pounds per capita; Kuwait, three; and Qatar, 2.5. Jordanians, who consume five pounds of coffee per capita, have zero Starbucks outlets.

Like every other business in the world, Starbucks has a specific clientele to which it appeals. For whatever reason, Starbucks is attractive not to all Arabs but rather to a particular sort of Arab. This is why Barber's imagined threat of monocultural, chain-driven sprawl across the face of the planet will never materialize. For anything like that to happen, there would have to be homogeneity of taste and thought. Starbucks will never assimilate the entire human race until we all have exactly the same wants and likes. In short, Barber has it backward. Material culture such as a Starbucks store doesn't create cultural conformity. It is cultural conformity—ideas and beliefs accepted individually, then shared by a group of likeminded individuals—that creates material culture.

What those worried about monoculture really fear is cross-cultural contamination: the dilution of foreign cultures by contact with America. But no culture is truly indigenous or untouched by others. Starbucks itself is an American repackaging of Italian coffee culture. The chain was originally indistinguishable from any other coffee shop. But in 1983 Starbucks chairman Howard Schultz (then head of marketing) took a business trip to Milan and was blown away by the grace and style—not to mention the coffee—of the city's 1,500 espresso bars.

Schultz eventually differentiated Starbucks from other American coffeehouses by modeling it on his Italian experience, with certain modifications to suit American tastes. These include chairs for loitering, jazz overhead instead of opera, and an Italian-sounding nonsense language (such as "frappuccino" and "tazo tea") that one ex-Starbucks exec freely admits was concocted in a boardroom. This just adds another stage in the international epic of coffee drinking: Starbucks customers, whether in Zurich or Beirut, are drinking an American version of an Italian evolution of a beverage invented by Arabs brewed from a bean discovered by Africans.

Anti-globalizers often ignore the fact that corporations are not charities giving away their products; they have customers who choose to buy their goods and services. Starbucks is "a mega-corporation destroying hundreds of mom-and-pop cafes," writes Stewart Lee Allen in his 1999 history of coffee, *The Devil's Cup*. "But that's just something large corporations do." No, that's just something consumers do—millions of them, making individual decisions every day. Personally, I tend to avoid Starbucks when I can. It has nothing to do with globalization or culture or politics or even coffee; the chain's tall-grande-venti menu simply presents too steep a learning curve for my small-medium-large brain. If others felt as I do, then Barber and his anti-globalization compadres would have their wish and Starbucks would vanish from the earth like the Ottomans did from the gates of Vienna. With 6,000 Starbucks in the world—and counting—the globe's coffee drinkers evidently feel differently. At least for now.

2

Winners and Losers: The Long-Range Effects of Outsourcing on U.S. Employment

John Cassidy

The long-range effects of outsourcing on U.S. employment and wages, coupled with the decline in American science graduates, means the U.S. must invest in its human capital to ensure our future prosperity.

N. Gregory Mankiw, the chairman of the White House Council of Economic Advisers, is a tall, mild-mannered Harvard scholar, widely admired within his profession for his sharp mind and clear exposition. He joined the Bush Administration last year, replacing Glenn Hubbard, who returned to Columbia University, and during his first nine months in Washington he attracted little attention, which suited him fine. However, in February, Mankiw found himself in the headlines after he described outsourcing—the shifting abroad of previously secure jobs, such as accounting and computer programming—as "the latest manifestation of the gains from trade that economists have talked about at least since Adam Smith." As

The New Yorker, August 2, 2004, v80, i21, p026.

Mankiw put it, "Outsourcing is just a new way of doing international trade. . . . More things are tradable than were tradable in the past and that's a good thing."

The response to these statements was immediate and bipartisan. Senator John Kerry, the Presidential candidate-elect, accused the White House of wishing "to export more of our jobs overseas." Tom Daschle, the Senate Democratic leader, claimed that President Bush and his advisers subscribed to "Alice-in-Wonderland economics." On the Republican side, Dennis Hastert, the Speaker of the House of Representatives, said Mankiw's "theory fails a basic test of economics," and Donald Manzullo, a congressman from Illinois, called for his resignation. Even the President seemed to disown Mankiw's words. "There are people looking for work because jobs have gone overseas," he said. "We need to act to make sure there are more jobs at home."

Shortly after receiving this public upbraiding, a chastened Mankiw spoke at a conference of economists, in Washington. He said that he had learned a valuable lesson: "Economists and non-economists speak very different languages. The two languages share many words in common, but they are often interpreted in different ways." Mankiw had a point. Put two economists in a room together and plain English is usually the first casualty. And yet the outcry his statements provoked cannot be dismissed as a linguistic misunderstanding. Although the number of people employed has picked up in recent months, the economy is still creating far fewer jobs than it did during previous cyclical upswings. According to the Bureau of Labor Statistics, non-farm employment peaked in March, 2001, at 132.5 million. In June, 2004, almost three years into an "economic recovery," total non-farm employment was 131.1 million. It is also an undisputed fact that many American businesses are choosing to relocate production to places like China and India, where there is ample cheap labor. I.B.M., for one, has confirmed that it is considering moving tens of thousands of jobs overseas to save money. In the past, manufacturing bore the brunt of this global labor arbitrage. Today, largely thanks to digitization and the Internet, the service sector, which employs fully four-fifths of the labor force, is increasingly affected. Many white-collar industries that once provided safe, well-paid employment, such as telecommunications, insurance, and stockbroking, are no longer immune from the temptation to outsource.

Well-educated American workers see software programmers in Bangalore earning six dollars an hour, when similarly trained domestic programmers are paid fifty or sixty dollars an hour, and, not surprisingly, they worry about their own livelihoods. Politicians are paid to reflect these concerns. As a senator, Kerry supported a host of free-trade initiatives, including the North American Free Trade Agreement and the extension of Most Favored Nation status to China. But once he embarked on a Presidential campaign he railed against "Benedict Arnold C.E.O.s" who transfer jobs overseas, and he proposed policies designed to limit outsourcing. Senator John Edwards, Kerry's running mate, has taken an even harder line. The Bush Administration, despite its ostensible support for trade liberalization, didn't hesitate to impose tariffs on foreign steel to protect domestic producers in swing states such as Ohio and West Virginia. The steel tariffs were eventually removed, after the European Union threatened a trade war, but the United States continues to provide hefty subsidies to dairy farmers, tobacco growers, and other agricultural producers.

Given these political realities, it is left to economists to defend free trade, which they tend to do without reservation, regardless of political affiliation. For example, one of Mankiw's predecessors, Martin N. Baily, who served in the Clinton Administration, has just co-authored a paper entitled "Exploding the Myths of Offshoring," which echoes Mankiw's arguments almost word for word. Despite Kerry's tough public stance, many of his economic advisers endorse views similar to Mankiw's and Baily's, as do the vast majority of economic commentators. During recent months, the *Wall Street Journal,* the *Financial Times, Business Week, Fortune,* and *The Economist* have each published articles pointing out the benefits of outsourcing. Only a few journalists have dared to challenge the received wisdom, most notably CNN's Lou Dobbs, who has been conducting a virulent populist attack on businesses that shift jobs overseas. Surely Dobbs, who left CNN for a while to work at Space.com, hasn't spotted something that the luminaries of the economics profession have missed?

Surprisingly enough, he might well have. While outsourcing isn't the only reason that businesses are so reluctant to hire American workers—rising productivity and a lack of faith in the recovery are others—it is certainly playing some role, a fact that corporate executives are much more willing to admit than economists are. Moreover, economists tend to overstate the theoretical case for outsourcing, arguing that trade liberalization is always and everywhere beneficial, which simply isn't true. In today's world, where multinational corporations can produce many goods and services practically anywhere, and where investment capital can move from one continent to another at the flick of a switch, there is no economic theory which guarantees that new types of trade, such as outsourcing, automatically benefit the United States. Some Americans gain: consumers, who enjoy lower prices; stockholders, who see profits rising at companies that employ cheap foreign labor. Some Americans lose: workers whose jobs are displaced; the owners of firms whose contracts are transferred to foreign suppliers. But the economists' argument that the country as a whole inevitably benefits is questionable.

As Mankiw indicated, it was Adam Smith who developed the argument that the unfettered exchange of goods and services allows individuals to specialize in what they do best, thereby raising over-all income and prosperity. "The taylor does not attempt to make his own shoes, but buys them of the shoemaker," Smith wrote in "The Wealth of Nations," which was published in 1776. "The shoemaker does not attempt to make his own clothes but employs a taylor." It may seem remarkable that economists still refer to the work of a Scottish radical who didn't even call himself an economist—his title at Glasgow University was professor of moral philosophy—but the division of labor, which is what Smith was talking about, lies at the heart of outsourcing and offshoring. (The two phrases once had distinct meanings, but now they are used interchangeably.)

Smith took the logic of specialization and applied it to the international market, arguing that no country should produce anything it could import more cheaply from abroad. "What is prudence in the conduct of every private family can scarcely be folly in that of a great kingdom," he wrote. This analysis implied that countries should concentrate on industries in which they are the low-cost producer, or, in the language of today's economists, industries in which they have an "absolute advantage" over foreign competitors.

A classic example involved Lancashire textile mills, which exploited the damp climate of northern England, and Portuguese vineyards, which prospered in the southern sun. In the presence of prohibitive tariffs on imports and exports, which were widespread at the time Smith was writing, England would have been forced to make its own wine (or go without), and Portugal would have had to manufacture cloth, which would have wasted valuable resources. But if free trade was introduced each country could concentrate on its strength, with England exchanging its surplus cloth for Portugal's surplus wine, to the benefit of consumers in both places.

The principle of absolute advantage is relatively easy to understand, and economists cite it all the time in an attempt to alleviate concerns about outsourcing. "The benefits from new forms of trade, such as in services, are no different from the benefits from traditional trade in goods," the Council of Economic Advisers said in its testimony to Congress earlier this year. "When a good or service is produced at lower cost in another country, it makes sense to import it rather than produce it domestically. This allows the United States to devote its resources to more productive purposes."

However, some types of offshoring are not so easy to rationalize. American insurance firms are hiring workers in countries like India to process customer claims. Yet many of the Americans who are being displaced are well-educated and productive employees who could probably do the job better than their Indian counterparts. Why, then, does this sort of trade benefit the United States? David Ricardo, another ancient British economist, answered this question in "Principles of Political Economy and Taxation," which was published in 1817, and it is his defense of free trade that Mankiw and his colleagues rely on to this day. Where Smith argued that nations gain by exporting goods which they can make more cheaply than other countries, Ricardo said that trade between countries makes sense even if one of the countries is the low-cost producer in every industry.

Suppose, he said, that in Portugal it takes ninety workers to make cloth and eighty workers to make wine, whereas in England cloth production requires a hundred workers and wine production requires a hundred and twenty. Then, assuming wages are the same in both countries, Portugal has an "absolute advantage" in wine and cloth. Should it still trade with England? Yes, said Ricardo. Compared with each other, he pointed out, Portugal's vineyards are still more efficient than its textile mills. Therefore, it makes sense for the country to specialize in wine production, export what it doesn't need, and import British cloth. Portugal's "comparative advantage" lies in wine.

Ricardo's argument is subtle—Paul Samuelson, the great M.I.T. economist, once said that comparative advantage is the most difficult economic theory to grasp—but it is also extremely powerful. It implies that the United States shouldn't try to keep hold of low-value businesses, such as insurance processing and telephone-call centers, even if its workers could operate them more efficiently than their counterparts in developing countries. Instead, it should concentrate on building up businesses like publishing and entertainment, where the displaced workers can be employed more productively. According to some estimates, the copyright business, which includes film, music, books, and software, accounts for about five per cent of the Gross Domestic Product, which means it is the biggest sector in the economy, bigger even than the auto industry. If the economists are to be believed, this is just as things should be: one industry that the United States used to dominate declines; another rises to take its place.

Any sensible discussion of trade has to acknowledge the power of comparative advantage. Capitalism has succeeded where other systems have failed in large part because it allows countries to develop according to its dictates. Poor places, like Mauritius and Indonesia, start out by producing labor-intensive goods, such as toys and clothing. Middle-income countries, such as South Korea and Taiwan, enter more advanced businesses, such as the manufacture of automobiles and consumer electronics. And developed nations, such as Japan and the United States, operate at the frontier of technology, creating industries like wireless communications and biotechnology. This hierarchy of production helps lift poor nations out of poverty. According to the World Bank, between 1981 and 2001 in East Asia the number of people living on less than a dollar a day, which is the bank's threshold for acute poverty, fell from about eight hundred million to less than three hundred million. This dramatic reduction would not have taken place if Thailand, Malaysia, and other Asian countries had been unable to export their products to the developed world.

But how does the rise of potential economic superpowers like China and India benefit the United States? Here, Ricardo's theory needs applying carefully. In a heretical but fascinating book, "Global Trade and Conflicting National Interests," which appeared in 2000, Ralph E. Gomory, the president of the Alfred P. Sloan Foundation, and William J. Baumol, an economist at N.Y.U., examined what happens when a low-wage economy begins competing with a high-wage economy. Unlike many economists, who tend to rely on make-believe models, Gomory and Baumol tried to be realistic. They assumed that export industries operate most efficiently on a large scale, which means that they tend to be concentrated in one region, and that countries can learn things from each other, such as how to assemble televisions and write software. The results of this analysis were startling. "If the wage differential between two trading countries is sufficiently large, the loss of industries to the low-wage, underdeveloped country may well benefit both countries at the national level," Gomory testified to Congress earlier this year. "However, as the underdeveloped country develops and starts to look more like the developed one, the balance turns around and further loss of industries becomes harmful to the overall welfare of the more developed nation."

This conclusion directly challenges Mankiw's claim that free trade must, as a matter of economic logic, benefit the United States. It supports the common-sense notion that what helps one nation can hurt another, and that countries adversely affected by foreign competition can lose out permanently. Although the work of Gomory and Baumol hasn't received much attention from other economists, and it certainly isn't the final word on the subject, it implies, at the very least, that the potential gains and losses from outsourcing need to be weighed.

In principle, it ought to be possible for the winners from free trade—consumers and stockholders, say—to compensate the losers with monetary benefits. In practice, such transfers rarely occur. Research by the Princeton economist Henry Farber, among others, shows that workers displaced by foreign competition are usually forced to take a pay cut, that is if they are fortunate enough to find new jobs. (The average cut is thirteen per cent.) Cities hit by plant closings take years to recover, and some—such as Gary, Indiana; Flint, Michigan; and Syracuse—never do.

The nearest thing to a compensation scheme is the federal Trade Adjustment Assistance program, which has recently been expanded. In 2003, this scheme provided income support and retraining grants to more than two hundred thousand displaced workers. However, a 2001 report by the General Accounting Office has shown that it is often ineffective, especially for older, less educated workers. Other ideas have been proposed, such as "wage insurance" for workers threatened by foreign competition, and tax credits for firms that invest in worker retraining, but with the budget deficit already approaching five hundred billion dollars their cost is prohibitive.

Although the Bush Administration beefed up the Trade Adjustment Assistance program, some of its members question the very idea of compensating the losers from trade. In a capitalist system, they point out, jobs are eliminated all the time, as a result of technical progress and shifting consumer tastes. Why, they ask, should the victims of trade get a better deal than the victims of a robot? Ben S. Bernanke, a Princeton economist and a member of the Federal Reserve Board, recently estimated that the American economy eliminates roughly fifteen million jobs a year—about one in seven of the total—as it redirects workers and resources to growing industries. By comparison, Ravi Aron, an economist at the Wharton School of Business, put the number of white-collar jobs lost to outsourcing between the start of 2000 and February of 2004 at about a hundred thousand a year. Other estimates, which include manufacturing, suggest that trade will eliminate perhaps three hundred and fifty thousand jobs this year. As Bernanke points out, even if this higher figure is correct, it implies that foreign competition accounts for only about one in fifty of all job losses.

That isn't the final analysis, however. Outsourcing service-sector jobs is a relatively new phenomenon, and it is growing fast. A widely cited example features Indian radiologists who examine X-rays from places like Miami and Chicago, and transmit their diagnoses via the Internet. It isn't hard to imagine other jobs that might be affected: reservation agents, telephone solicitors, computer programmers, accountants, database managers, financial analysts, and anybody else who performs easily replicable tasks with the aid of a computer. The jobs that are likely to remain safe are those which require physical proximity and intellectual flexibility, such as nursing, plumbing, social work, and teaching.

One report, from Forrester Research, a technology consulting firm in Cambridge, Massachusetts, suggested that between now and 2015 about 3.3 million white-collar positions will shift abroad. Outsourcing of manufacturing jobs is also on the rise. According to Economy.com, a research firm based in West Chester, Pennsylvania, taking service industries and manufacturing together, the number of jobs moving overseas will reach six hundred thousand a year by 2010. Predictions of this nature should be regarded as educated guesswork, but they illustrate that concern about outsourcing isn't a passing fad—a situation that at least some mainstream economists are willing to acknowledge.

"A huge, new swatch of our jobs will become vulnerable to foreign competition over the next few years," Berkeley's J. Bradford DeLong and Stephen S. Cohen wrote in an article that DeLong recently posted on his Web site. "This new set of potentially tradeable jobs are in many cases held by people who are not accustomed to layoffs. Often, they are high-paying, clean, good jobs. Some are the best jobs. The people who hold them are quite convinced that they are on top—that they have these jobs and that these jobs are well-paying—because they are the best people who deserve to have them; they are smart and industrious."

Some economists privately acknowledge that the arguments about outsourcing are nuanced, but they fear that any weakening of support for free trade could do untold damage to the economy. During the Great Depression, Congress introduced the infamous Smoot-Hawley Tariff Act, which raised duties on a range of foreign goods. Other countries retaliated, and the subsequent downturn in international trade intensified the slump. The economists are right when they say protectionism isn't the answer to outsourcing. But they need to get beyond pat slogans about free trade.

John Kerry has at least tried to address the issue. His outsourcing plan, which was largely drawn up by Jason Furman, a young economist who was formerly one of Mankiw's students at Harvard, would revoke tax breaks for companies that shift production overseas and redistribute some of the extra revenue in the form of subsidies to firms that expand hiring in the United States. Politically, this proposal is an astute response to popular concern about outsourcing. Practically, it is unlikely to have much impact. All too often, the cost reductions that firms enjoy by moving jobs abroad are so large that hitting them with a tax increase wouldn't make much difference to their calculations.

And employment subsidies often end up benefitting workers who would have been hired anyway.

There is another issue, which hasn't been addressed. At the moment, the outsourcing debate is focussed on jobs and employment security. Soon, it will revolve around wages and benefits as well. Ultimately, it is the level of demand in the economy, not trade policy, that dictates the pace of job creation. As long as the Federal Reserve and Congress utilize monetary and fiscal policies effectively to keep up spending, the economy should eventually create enough jobs of some sort to occupy most people who want to work. But what sort of pay will they command? A long-established theorem of international economics—the "factor-price equalization theorem"—states that when two countries start out with similar technology and skills but different wage rates, trade between them will reduce wages in the high-paying country and increase wages in the low-paying country until, eventually, workers in both places end up earning the same amount.

Until now, most American workers have been able to escape this pincer movement, but as countries like China and India fulfill their potential this may change. More and more American workers will be forced to compete with poorly paid labor in the developing world, and the downward pressure on American wages could become irresistible. In the nineteen-seventies, when Asian manufacturers targeted their American rivals, Japanese wages were about half of American wages, and the resultant competition was one reason that workers' earnings stagnated for a generation. Today, workers in India earn between a fifth and a tenth as much as their American counterparts. "On the one hand, economists will say that the gains from trade will thereby be that much greater for the economy as a whole," DeLong and Cohen write. "On the other hand, the potential downward pressure on loser workers in rich countries will be that much greater as well."

Some industries that compete internationally, such as pharmaceuticals and avionics, have succeeded despite paying their workers high wages, because the United States has maintained an edge in science and technology. But the ongoing transfer of knowledge and expertise to developing countries, as well as changing attitudes toward business and entrepreneurship in those societies, means American leadership can no longer be taken for granted.

The essential point is that comparative advantage is no longer endowed by nature: through hard work and enlightened administration, countries can wrest it from each other's grasp. Ricardo was writing about economies dominated by agriculture and rudimentary manufacturing, where a favorable climate and the ready availability of raw materials were vital. These days, the keys to economic success are a well-educated workforce, technical know-how, high levels of capital investment, and entrepreneurial zeal—all of which countries can acquire with the help of supportive governments, multinational firms, and international investors.

A couple of months ago, the *Times* reported that the United States is losing its dominance in basic scientific research, reflected in the fact that the proportion of American articles in a number of top physics journals fell from sixty-one per cent in 1983 to twenty-nine per cent in 2003. This decline reflects disturbing trends throughout the education system. Indian colleges, with their strong programs in science and math, are producing more than forty thousand graduates in computer science a year, with enrollment increasing all the time. In the United States, meanwhile, many colleges are struggling to fill their science programs, and high-school dropout rates are higher than they were thirty-five years ago. In 1969, 77.1 per cent of seventeen-year-olds graduated; in 2002, the most recent year for which statistics are available, the figure was 72.5 per cent. As Pedro Carneiro, a lecturer at University College, London, and James J. Heckman, a professor at the University of Chicago, pointed out in a recent paper, "By many measures, since 1980, the quality of the U.S. workforce has stagnated, or its growth has slowed down dramatically."

If the United States is to meet the challenge posed by a truly global economy, it will have to insure that its scientists are the most creative, its business leaders the most innovative, and its workers the most highly skilled—not easy when other nations are seeking the same goals. A truly enlightened trade policy would involve increasing federal support for science at all levels of the education system; creating financial incentives for firms to pursue technological innovation; building up pre-school and mentoring initiatives that reduce dropout rates; expanding scholarships and visas to attract able foreign students and entrepreneurs to these shores; and encouraging the development of the arts. In short, insuring our prosperity involves investing in our human, social, and cultural capital. But don't expect to see that slogan on a campaign bumper sticker anytime soon.

3

Dietary Patterns
and Acculturation

Dietary habits in the United States

Migration and acculturation are associated with changes in chronic disease risk. Epidemiologic studies consistently show that people who migrate from one part of the world to another quickly adopt the chronic disease patterns of their new host country. For example, Japanese immigrants to Hawaii experience a 50% decrease in stomach cancer risk, but a three-fold increase in breast cancer risk after just one generation. Japanese and Mexican immigrants living in the United States have higher rates of cardiovascular disease compared with those living in their home countries. The prevalence of hypertension is higher among African-Americans who have lived in the United States for several generations compared with first-generation immigrants. An important ethnic group in which to examine migration-related changes in diet and other lifestyle habits is Hispanics, because they are the fastest growing ethnic group in the United States. The objective of the present study was to examine the associations of acculturation with diet in a homogeneous sample of Hispanics, and to investigate whether acculturation is an independent predictor of fruit, vegetable and fat intake among Hispanics living in Washington State.

Data are from Celebrating Health!, a community intervention trial in the Yakima Valley of central Washington state. The overall objective of the trial is to assess the effectiveness of a comprehensive cancer prevention program, including a dietary intervention. Approximately 50% of the Yakima Valley Population is Hispanic, 90% of whom are from Michoacan, Mexico. Residents

Nutrition Research Newsletter, Feb 2004, v23, i2, p13(1).

were recruited for an in-person baseline survey to obtain information about health beliefs and practices, diet, acculturation, and demographics. From a sample of 2,862 addresses, 2,345 were approached for study participation. There were 1,795 interviews completed.

Usual fruit and vegetable consumption during the previous month was assessed with a modified version of the instruments used in the Behavioral Risk Factor Surveillance System and the National 5-A-Day for Better Health program. These questionnaires contain six items that estimate the frequency of consumption of fruit, 100% fruit juice, and vegetables. Fat intake was assessed with the Fat-Related Diet Habits questionnaire. This 12-item questionnaire asks about diet over the previous month and assesses avoiding fat as flavoring, substituting specially flavored manufactured low-fat foods, modifying meals to be lower in fat, replacing high-fat foods with fruits and vegetables, and avoiding fried foods.

Dietary patterns varied by ethnicity and acculturation status. On average, compared with non-Hispanic white residents, Hispanics consumed one more serving of fruits and vegetables per day. Dietary habits changed as Hispanics acculturated to the United States. Highly acculturated Hispanics ate fewer servings of fruits and vegetables per day, compared with those not highly acculturated. Highly acculturated Hispanics had slightly higher—but not statistically significant—scores on the Fat-Related Diet Habits questionnaire, which corresponds to a higher fat intake, compared with low-acculturated Hispanics. The early dietary changes made on acculturation included adding fat at the table to breads and potatoes.

The findings of this study support the hypothesis that acculturation is an independent predictor of diet. Nutrition professionals should encourage their Hispanic clients to maintain their traditional dietary practices, such as the high intakes of fruits and vegetables, and to eat bread and potatoes without added fat. Dietitians can provide information about fat reduction behaviors that may be novel to recent immigrants, such as the use of reduced-fat milk or other lower-fat items.

4

Origin of Species

Thomas L. Friedman

Two basic responses to globalization: Infosys and Al Qaeda

N andan Nilekani, C.E.O. of the Indian software giant Infosys, gave me a
tour the other day of his company's wood-paneled global conference
room in Bangalore. It looks a lot like a beautiful tiered classroom, with
a massive wall-size screen at one end and cameras in the ceiling so that Infosys
can hold a simultaneous global teleconference with its U.S. innovators, its
Indian software designers and its Asian manufacturers. "We can have our
whole global supply chain on the screen at the same time," holding a virtual
meeting, explained Mr. Nilekani. The room's eight clocks tell the story: U.S.
West, U.S. East, G.M.T., India, Singapore, Hong Kong, Japan, Australia.

As I looked at this, a thought popped into my head: Who else has such a
global supply chain today? Of course: Al Qaeda. Indeed, these are the two
basic responses to globalization: Infosys and Al Qaeda.

Infosys said all the walls have been blown away in the world, so now we,
an Indian software company, can use the Internet, fiber optic telecommunications and e-mail to get superempowered and compete anywhere that our
smarts and energy can take us. And we can be part of a global supply chain
that produces profit for Indians, Americans and Asians.

Al Qaeda said all the walls have been blown away in the world, thereby
threatening our Islamic culture and religious norms and humiliating some of
our people, who feel left behind. But we can use the Internet, fiber optic
telecommunications and e-mail to develop a global supply chain of angry

The New York Times, March 14, 2004 pWK13, col 01, (17 col in).

© 2004 The New York Times Company. Reprinted with permission.

people that will superempower us and allow us to hit back at the Western civilization that's now right in our face.

"From the primordial swamps of globalization have emerged two genetic variants," said Mr. Nilekani. "Our focus therefore has to be how we can encourage more of the good mutations and keep out the bad."

Indeed, it is worth asking what are the spawning grounds for each. Infosys was spawned in India, a country with few natural resources and a terrible climate. But India has a free market, a flawed but functioning democracy and a culture that prizes education, science and rationality, where women are empowered. The Indian spawning ground rewards anyone with a good idea, which is why the richest man in India is a Muslim software innovator, Azim Premji, the thoughtful chairman of Wipro.

Al Qaeda was spawned in Saudi Arabia, Pakistan and Afghanistan, societies where there was no democracy and where fundamentalists have often suffocated women and intellectuals who crave science, free thinking and rationality. Indeed, all three countries produced strains of Al Qaeda, despite Pakistan's having received billions in U.S. aid and Saudi Arabia's having earned billions from oil. But without a context encouraging freedom of thought, women's empowerment and innovation, neither society can tap and nurture its people's creative potential—so their biggest emotional export today is anger.

India, Pakistan, Saudi Arabia and Afghanistan each spontaneously generated centers for their young people's energies. In India they're called "call centers," where young men and women get their first jobs and technical skills servicing the global economy and calling the world. In Pakistan, Afghanistan and Saudi Arabia they're called "madrassas," where young men, and only young men, spend their days memorizing the Koran and calling only God. Ironically, U.S. consumers help to finance both. We finance the madrassas by driving big cars and sending the money to Saudi Arabia, which uses it to build the madrassas that are central to Al Qaeda's global supply chain. And we finance the call centers by consuming modern technologies that need backup support, which is the role Infosys plays in the global supply chain.

Both Infosys and Al Qaeda challenge America: Infosys by competing for U.S. jobs through outsourcing, and Al Qaeda by threatening U.S. lives through terrorism. As Michael Mandelbaum, the Johns Hopkins foreign policy professor, put it: "Our next election will be about these two challenges—with the Republicans focused on how we respond to Al Qaeda, and the losers from globalization, and the Democrats focused on how we respond to Infosys, and the winners from globalization."

Every once in a while the technology and terrorist supply chains intersect—like last week. Reuters quoted a Spanish official as saying after the Madrid train bombings: "The hardest thing [for the rescue workers] was hearing mobile phones ringing in the pockets of the bodies. They couldn't get that out of their heads."

5

Religions and Globalisation

Peter L. Berger

The topic I propose to address here is vast, and all I can reasonably do is to present a picture painted with very large brushstrokes. Much of what I will have to say will be based on insights gained from the work of the research centre I direct at Boston University, first of all from the largest project we ever undertook—a ten-country study of globalisation and culture (the major results have been published in a volume I co-edited with Samuel Huntington, *Many Globalisations: Cultural Diversity in the Contemporary World* Oxford University Press, 2002). And before I say anything about religion, I must make some general observations about the cultural dimension of globalisation. (Though I will point out right away that in most of the world, as soon as one looks at culture, one is looking at religion.)

Globalisation is a process driven by immensely powerful economic and technological forces. We know that there are both benefits and costs, material and other, resulting from this process, both between and within societies. I cannot deal with this aspect of the matter here, important though it is. But there is one rather simple fact to be noted: globalisation means an enormous increase in the possibilities of communication between an increasing number of people throughout the world. With less and less effort, everyone can talk with everyone else. This is true not only of people sitting at the levers of economic and political power, but of people in every other institution—academics, advocates of religious or ideological messages, gangsters, aficionados of every type of hobby from stamp-collecting to pornography—and, increasingly, ordinary people with the money to travel or with access to telephones, fax machines or modems. It seems to me that this basic fact is worth thinking about for a moment, because it already makes it very implausible to evaluate this global chatterbox as either all good or all bad. One may rejoice at the ease with which university professors or stamp-collectors in Boston can communicate with their colleagues in Bangkok, but the joy will be tempered by the recognition that drug-lords, terrorists and paedophiles share this facility.

European Judaism, Spring 2003, v36, i1, p4(7).

There is by now a conventional view of the relation between globalisation and culture, a view which is shared by both proponents and critics of globalisation. This view holds that there is an emerging global culture, most of it Western and indeed American both in origin and content, and further that this culture is rolling across the world like a gigantic steamroller. For some, there is a great hope there—a global culture that will promote higher standards of living, an international civil society and democracy. Others look at this culture as a great threat—at best, as the spread of superficial and trivial ways of life, at worst as an evil conspiracy of neo-imperialists in the service of a predatory capitalism. I think that both the hope and the threat are greatly exaggerated. In any case, the cultural situation (be it perceived favourably or not) is considerably more complicated.

Like many conventional views, this one has some basis in fact. There is indeed an emerging global culture, mainly Western and American in inspiration. It has both elite and popular manifestations—in the international business elite which Samuel Huntington felicitously called the "Davos culture", but also in other elites (including a globalised intelligentsia)—but through popular culture it penetrates vastly larger populations. In all these manifestations a significant fact is the near-absolute hegemony of the English language, and of American English at that. I will only remark here that one does not use a language innocently; like it or not, one takes on board a heavy freight of cognitive and normative assumptions which come with the language.

Talk about a global culture is relatively recent. But the phenomenon relates to something that has been talked about for a much longer time—namely, the process of modernisation. That too has its origins in the West, though these go back to a time when America was less important on the world stage. Whatever else it may be, the emerging global culture is modernising. It perceives itself and is perceived by others, correctly so, as distinctively modern and thus in tension with, if not in opposition to, traditional beliefs, values and lifestyles. The young, upwardly mobile African, who grooms himself for a job in a multinational corporation—the provincial Chinese bureaucrat who applies for a visiting fellowship to the United States—but also the teenager in Vladivostok who knows all the latest rock stars, dances to their music and wears T-shirts with the names of American universities—all these individuals are aspirants to a modern lifestyle and, at least in part, a modern worldview. It is also plausible to say that these individuals are candidates for fuller participation in modern economic and political institutions. One aspect of modernisation which is particularly relevant here is that of individuation: for reasons that I cannot possibly go into here, the modernisation process tends to take the individual out of taken-for-granted traditional identities and throws him or her on his or her own resources. The emerging global culture, be it on elite or popular levels, provides a context that makes this potentially wrenching transition meaningful and bearable.

Thus far, what I have said does not necessarily contradict the conventional view. As one looks more closely, however, that view has to be considerably modified. Generally speaking, the emerging global culture is not inexorable (that is, it is not a steamroller), it is not monolithic, and it is not irreversible.

People can resist it or modify it. And they may pick and choose between conflicting elements within it. To make the last point just very briefly: the same process of cultural globalisation transports the "Washington consensus" and its Western critics, rap images of promiscuous sexuality along with feminist ideology and Christian Evangelical notions of virtue, calorie-rich fast-food and health fads, and so on.

But let me emphasise the non-inexorable character of the global culture. To be sure, there is one response to the global culture that can only be described as supine. Not long ago I attended a workshop in Europe for employees of a multinational firm of business consultants. The language, of course, was English. The participants came from all comers of the world, all highly motivated and promising young members of the "Davos culture". Except for different shades of skin pigmentation, it was impossible to tell who came from where. They looked alike, dressed alike, talked alike, laughed at the same jokes, had the same body language. Now, it is possible that some of them went home to some exotic locale after the workshop, donned native garb and participated in ancient tribal rituals. But in this particular case I would doubt it. I spent time with them after the formal sessions, and the impression I obtained was that these were people who were thoroughly socialised, in behaviour as well as consciousness, into the global culture which was well represented by their employer. (I might add that I did not find these people very attractive.)

The same global culture, however, can also be passionately even violently rejected. There is a spectrum of responses here —from the superior contempt of European intellectuals (I recall the description of the European branch of Disneyland, by a former French government minister, as a "cultural Chernobyl"), to the riots that now routinely accompany meetings of the World Bank and similar organisations, all the way to the terrorism of Islamic militants. It does not need emphasis that this is a very serious phenomenon, but I have no particularly useful comments about it to make here. What I find both interesting and important is the responses that fall between supine acceptance and violent rejection. I will give only one example, and with it I will have arrived at the subject of religion.

We came upon it in our aforementioned project, part of which was a study of people in the computer industry in India. Here are people who are as modernised as any in the world. Yet many of them are pious Hindus, who practise traditional rituals and who take caste seriously. And at least some of them seem to manage, without visible tension, their living in both the world of global business and technology and the world of traditional Hinduism. One image to make the point: there is a Hindu festival during which artisans put garlands on their tools and worship these as instruments of divine creativity. The festival is celebrated in some firms in Bangalore by putting garlands on the computers. This raises a very interesting issue indeed: what the Israeli sociologist Samuel Eisenstadt, among others, has called the possibility of alternate modernities. The Western modernity transported by the global culture is not the only possible one. What is happening in different parts of the world is that people, often with great ingenuity, are trying and often succeeding in blending Western-derived modernity with elements of traditional culture. It seems to me that this is a very positive development, and religion plays an important part in it.

Let me now discuss briefly what are arguably the two most dynamic religious movements in the world today—first, what can loosely be called "popular Protestantism"—and then resurgent Islam.

The core of the first movement is the worldwide explosion of Pentecostalism. This is so alien to Western academics and media people that, despite its immense dimensions, it took some time before it was widely noticed. The British sociologist David Martin, who has studied this phenomenon for many years, estimates that there are at least 250 million Pentecostals in the world and possibly as many more (the big question mark is China, where much of this movement takes place underground). Our research centre supported Martin's first project, which was in Latin America, and there it has become very clear that Pentecostalism constitutes nothing less than a cultural revolution (there are now about 50 million Pentecostals south of the Rio Grande)—in attitudes to work and education, in the status of women, in personal behaviour both inside and outside the family. I agree with Martin that this cultural transformation is inherently modernising—indeed, it replicates the "Protestant ethic" analysed by Marx Weber—and that it also should be seen as a popular dimension of the emerging global culture, though with significant modifications. It very visibly continues a religious movement that originated in the United States in the first years of the twentieth century, but it also blends with cultural components indigenous to Latin America. The heaviest concentration of Pentecostals (for reasons I don't fully understand) is in Guatemala—at least 25% of the population by now—and there one finds people singing American Gospel hymns translated into the Mayan language.

"Popular Protestantism" includes groups other than Pentecostals—various Christian Evangelical groups that are not Pentecostal, Mormons, Jehovah's Witnesses, the so-called African Initiated Churches—all of them successfully spreading in some countries. Whatever one may think of their religious beliefs and practices (perhaps I should interject here that I am a Lutheran, though not a very orthodox one, and that I'm not personally tempted by any of them), I would propose that we can see here cases of successful alternate modernities, albeit still on a very unsophisticated level. Increasingly, these groups have created global networks, transporting people and ideas across the world.

Resurgent Islam, and by no means only in its more militant factions, has also become a globalising movement. The Muslim diaspora in the West, especially in Europe, plays a strategic role here. There is a widely diffused theme of opposition to the global culture, as famously expressed in Khomeini's characterisation of America (and by implication of the West as a whole) as the "Great Satan". (It is worth reflecting on the fact that, both in the Bible and the Quran, Satan is depicted as the great tempter. Western culture may be the enemy, but it is also the great temptation.)

I think it is fair to say that Islam, unlike Protestantism, has much greater difficulties adapting to modernity. I suspect that an important factor in this is the status of women as between the two religions. But, be this as it may, there are important Islamic movements that are credibly seeking to construct an alternate modernity—in the Arab word, in Turkey, even among clerical circles in Iran. The most important movements, though, are to be found in Indonesia—as the most populous Muslim country, hardly a marginal case. Both the two major Islamic movements, Nudhat'ul-Ulama and Muhammadiya (each with millions of adherents), represent an understanding of the relation between Islam and modernity far removed from that of militants in the Middle East. My colleague Robert Hefner (an associate director of our research centre), in his recent book on Indonesia, uses the term "civil Islam" to describe these movements, specifically the first-named one. Its leader, Abdurrahman Wahid, has eloquently spoken about his vision of such an Islam—pro-democracy, pro-market-economy, in favour of religious liberty, the equality of women, and the separation of the state from the religious law—yet decidedly Muslim in belief, ritual and morality. Wahid is a very impressive intellectual. It is a great pity that he is not a clever politician. The failure of his short-lived presidency is a setback for "civil Islam"—a successful presidency would have given him a great "bully pulpit"—but he is still very much around, and 1 would consider him as a living example of how an Islamic alternate modernity can be envisaged.

Everyone is talking with everyone else: Campus Crusade for Christ, an American Christian Evangelical group, screens its "Jesus Movie" in dubbed-in indigenous languages in dozens of countries. More people attend mosques in England every week than attend Anglican services. Monumental Mormon temples have gone up just outside the Buenos Aires airport and across from the University of the Witwatersrand in Johannesburg (and, don't ask me why, the most numerous conversions to Mormonism have occurred in the South Pacific). Devotees of Krishna dance and sing on the streets of cities throughout America and Europe. Followers of Lubavitch Hasidism, whose headquarters are in Brooklyn, are reviving Judaism in Russia. And so on.

Virtually all religious communities are today, if not globalising, reaching across the borders of their traditional territories. But they differ in their intention or capacity to create new forms of modernity. The Roman Catholic Church, of course, has been a global institution for centuries. So the fact that it is so now is hardly newsworthy. What is interesting is various attempts to relate Catholicism to modernity in new ways. Opus Dei is an important case in point. While rigorously orthodox in its doctrine and piety, it has shown remarkable flexibility in adapting to the modern world. In Spain, its country of origin, it played an important role in the transition to a modern market economy, and at least an indirect role in the transition to democracy in the wake of the Franco regime. It continues to be very influential in various Latin American countries and in the Philippines. It represents an interesting case of a project for an alternate modernity. All the major Protestant groups engage in exercises of global outreach, with varying degrees of success. The effects of this are sometimes unexpected. The faces of the Anglican bishops who gather periodically for the Lambeth conferences are increasingly non-white—Anglicanism is in pretty bad shape in England and not much better in America, but it is doing well in Africa. Liberal white churchmen have been happy about this multiculturalism. They have become less happy when they discovered that these African bishops do not share their progressive views on such topics as abortion or homosexuality. Eastern Christian Orthodoxy is probably the least globalising of major Christian communities, but the revival of religion in Russia has included people who seek a path to modernity that would not simply replicate that of the West. Some of these efforts, unfortunately, have some ugly nationalistic undertones.

A major case of religious globalisation is constituted by the inroads of south- and east-Asian religiosity in the West. Tulasi Srinivas, an anthropologist who headed the India portion of our globalisation project, coined the term "counter-emissions", by which she means cultural influences going from east to west, rather than the other way. The British sociologist Colin Campbell uses the term "Easternisation" to describe the same phenomenon. Hinduism, despite some efforts in this direction (such as the Hare Krishna and the Sal Baba movements, and, on a more sophisticated level, the much older Ramakrishna Mission and the Vedanta Society), has not been very successful in this. The Hindu diaspora in the West is largely ethnic in composition, but the attempts to combine Hinduism with an assimilated lifestyle are also interesting under the rubric of alternate modernity. Buddhism is the more visible case of a religious "counter-emission". The majority of Buddhists in America is still composed of Asian immigrants, but there are estimates of about 800,000 non-ethnic converts. If one picks up Buddhist periodicals, one finds fascinating discussions of just what it means to be an American Buddhist—discussions of which traditional Buddhist doctrines and practices are indispensable, as against those that could be given up in the service of indigenisation. Campbell has been particularly interested in so-called New Age religiosity, an unorganised yet very important influx of Asian ideas and practices into the West.

At the moment I am especially interested in the aforementioned African Initiated Churches, because we are planning a research project on the economic and political behaviour of their members. These churches are highly syncretistic, combining Christianity with various elements of traditional African religion. We have relatively few data on this as yet, but anecdotal evidence is to the effect that, while their religious beliefs and practices may seem outlandish or suspect to Western theologians, their morality, like the Pentecostals', conforms to the modernising "Protestant ethic". Millions of people belong to these churches in sub-Saharan Africa, potentially an enormously significant social force. Thabo Mbeki, the president of South Africa, has been speaking of an "African Renaissance", a distinctively African path to modernity. I don't think that he had the African Initiated Churches in mind. It would be intriguing if they turned out to be an important agent of such a cultural transformation.

I must come to an end here. I have touched on many subjects, each of which would require much more detailed discussion. But I hope that I have made two points: That the relations between globalisation and culture are quite complex. And that religion is a very important aspect of these relations.

6

For Native Alaskans, Tradition Is Yielding to Modern Customs

Sarah Kershaw

Native Alaskan tribes such as the Siberian Yupiks worry that their cultural traditions are disappearing

When it became clear that the elders in this isolated Eskimo village on St. Lawrence Island in the Bering Sea approved of the marriage, Clifford Apatiki's relatives did what was required of them: They bought him his bride.

That meant, according to a fast-fading custom here among the Siberian Yupiks, a small but sturdy native Alaskan tribe that has inhabited this treeless and brutally windy island since about A.D. 500, that Mr. Apatiki's family would spend at least a year coming up with the payment. They called on their relatives, here in Gambell, over in Savoonga, the other Yupik village on this island 38 miles from the Chukchi peninsula in Russia, and across Alaska, to send them things—sealskins, rifles, bread, a toaster, a house full of gifts.

When the bride's family accepted the offerings, Mr. Apatiki, a skilled ivory carver and polar bear hunter, did what was required of him: he went to work for her family as a kind of indentured servant for a year, hunting seal, whale and polar bear, and doing chores.

The marriage between Mr. Apatiki, 30, and the former Jennifer Campbell, 29, who was a bookkeeper for the village tribal council, was formalized five

The New York Times, August 21, 2004, pA1, col 01, (43 col in).

years ago, when traditional marriages such as theirs were still the norm here.
But now the couple worry whether their children will follow suit because
even in five years this and other centuries-old traditions in this village of 700
have been slipping away, as one of the most remote villages on earth finally
contends with the modern world.

"I'm sure people will continue to do it for a while," Mrs. Apatiki said one
evening in the living room of her one-story home in the village. "If the tradition isn't in effect with some families, they are whispered about. They will say
about a girl, 'She was not bought.'"

Still, it is of great concern to the elders in Gambell that this marriage
tradition is disappearing in the face of whirlwind change here over the last
decade. Life has shifted so much in Gambell, where satellite television, rising
rates of alcoholism and a growing rejection by the younger generation of the
Yupik language and customs have begun to chip away at tradition and at a
hunting-and-gathering subsistence lifestyle, that it is as if the world here is
playing on videotape stuck on fast-forward.

And fewer couples are getting married in the traditional way, despite pleas
from their parents and grandparents in this whaling community. The rising
tension between the old ways and the new ones, between older generations
and younger ones, is playing out in native villages across this state, where
16 percent of the population is native Alaskan, comprising 11 distinct cultures
and speaking 20 different languages. The Internet, much more regular airline
travel and other modern advances are connecting even the most remote
Alaskan villages to mainstream society.

"Gambell, it has changed quite a bit now," said Winfred James, 82, one of
the village's most knowledgeable elders, one recent evening in his living room,
where he was watching a CNN interview with Senator John Kerry and his
wife. "Westernization is coming in."

Mr. James said he and other elders were deeply concerned about losing
the marriage customs, "but it probably will change with the next generation."

"We try to teach them to do that, you know," he added. "So they can
know each other, so they can stick together."

Village residents say that more and more young couples are simply living
together and not pursuing the traditional marriage customs or that men are
working for the families of their fiancees for much shorter periods, if at all.

"They work for maybe a month, and then I guess they forget," said
Christopher Koonooka, 26, who teaches at the village school in a bilingual program. Mr. Koonooka said he saw many of his peers rejecting the old traditions.

The Siberian Yupiks inhabit Gambell and Savoonga, another village of
700 people about 50 miles from here, and parts of the Siberian Chukchi
Peninsula, where about 900 Siberian Yupiks live. Gambell was named after a
Presbyterian missionary, Vene Gambell, who came to St. Lawrence Island in
the late 1800's. He was followed by other missionaries, whose Western-
sounding surnames made their way into the lineage of the Yupiks.

The first working telephones were installed here in the 1970's, and television was not readily available until about a decade ago; running water became

available to about half of the homes here about five years ago. Before satellite television, Gambell residents watched the news at least two weeks late on videotapes flown in with other supplies from Nome, the closest city on the Alaska mainland, 200 miles away and reachable only by small plane.

Almost every house has a satellite dish, and the first cellular telephone tower was built, near the one-room trailer that serves as the police station, a few years ago.

The people here generally welcome much of the technology even as the village elders and others say television is a particularly disturbing force.

For example, Global Positioning Systems now provide great assistance to hunters who could might otherwise get terribly lost in the rough Bering Sea, especially because some of the old knowledge about how to find the whales, seals and walrus has been lost.

And the Internet has not only allowed greater access to information, but ivory carvers, who would otherwise have to wait for the occasional tourist or birder, use it to advertise and sell their wares. (Only the hardiest birders make the trek out here from Nome, and tourists arrive only once in a while, on cruise ships that sometimes stop on the shores of Gambell.)

"Technology has had a big impact, in good ways and bad ways," said Mattox Metcalf, high school program art coordinator for the Alaska Native Heritage Center in Anchorage and a Siberian Yupik who was born in Gambell. "Some of my relatives have said they are competing hard with what's on T.V."

"The younger people are seeing stuff on T.V., and they are slowly realizing that what they do is different from what other people do in the U.S.," said Mr. Metcalf, 24, who travels here frequently to visit relatives. "And they want to be like them. The older people are trying to fight for their minds and fight for their attention. It is kind of at a stalemate right now."

Carol Zane Jolles, an anthropologist at the University of Washington who has studied the people of St. Lawrence Island and recently published a book about her research, said she had seen radical changes here, even since she first visited in the late 1980's. Returning in the last few years, Dr. Jolles was struck, she said, by how children were speaking English first with each other, rather than Siberian Yupik, the main language of their parents, and that she saw major shifts in the marriage customs and in family structure.

In a society still structured around clans, the recent construction of modern houses has shifted the emphasis from the extended family to the nuclear family, she said. The newer homes, pre-fabricated and shipped here, replaced the small driftwood and walrus-hide houses that still stand in the older part of the village, where dozens of people live and there is no running water.

"Everyone now has access to the way the rest of the world lives," Dr. Jolles said. "They are American citizens and they have the same interests and values."

She added, "They are watching how other people live on television, the modern movies, and there is a great impact on young people."

As much as things have changed in Gambell, there are some constants, and on a recent summer afternoon, life, on the surface anyway, was unfolding much as it has for hundreds of years.

Split walrus skins, used to cover and waterproof the hunting boats, were stretched across wooden planks, drying out under the sun. Some of the women were picking greens up on the mountain, preparing to soak them in tall buckets of mountain spring water and store them for the winter. In the winter, the rocky mountain is bare, except for gravestones and above-ground coffins in the village cemetery and piles of snow. There are greens and berries to be harvested here in the summer and sea fruits wash up on the beach in the fall, but no fruits or vegetables can be found in the winter.

Other women were picking through the cache of meat carved from a 40-foot bowhead whale caught last April, contemplating dinner. The meat is kept in hand-made freezers dug out in the still frosty tundra, on a foggy landscape scattered with giant whalebones, prized trophies laid across the black gravel. Later that night, the women sliced up the whale blubber and served it on a large tray, along with bits of smoked seal and walrus flippers, a delicacy, at a party for a couple celebrating their 17th wedding anniversary.

The men, meanwhile, including Kenneth James, 24, the grandson of Winfred James and an up-and-coming whale, walrus and reindeer hunter, were checking their nets for salmon and trout, zooming back and forth between their one-story wooden houses and the beach on all-terrain vehicles that, in the summer, replace snowmobiles as the only mode of transportation in this roadless village. Others were buffing and polishing their intricate walrus ivory carvings.

Kenneth James, perhaps one of the last to abide by the marriage tradition, will soon begin working for his girlfriend's family, once his grandfather gathers an acceptable amount of goods for them.

He was stoic about his duty.

"I will be going to work soon," Mr. James said late one evening, as the sun, which does not set here in the summer until 2 a.m., was still lighting up the village.

He was eager to hop on his all-terrain vehicle and check his salmon nets.

"It's what I will do," he said.

This evidence that some young people are still keeping the marriage tradition makes many elders happy.

Perhaps the Gambell resident most concerned about what the village is facing these days is Edmond Apassingok, 41, president of the Indian Reorganization Act Council, which, along with the Gambell City Council, governs the village.

Mr. Apassingok, a whale hunter who caught a 50-foot whale last January (the meat is shared among all the residents and catching a whale is cause for a huge, emotional celebration) is deeply concerned about the rising temperatures in Alaska, he said. The climatic change, the annual mean temperature has risen in Alaska 5.4 degrees over the last 30 years, has shortened the season for whale hunting because the ice that provides the right conditions for the whales has begun to melt earlier in the spring.

But Mr. Apassingok has other worries, as well.

"Every generation is losing something," he said.

7

India's Outsourcing Boom

Rebecca Fannin

Sure, the infrastructure is bad. But India's huge labor pool suggests the growth may last.

The bumpy roads leading to Bangalore's Electronics City are thronged with rickshaws, overcrowded buses, mopeds, noisy old trucks, ox-drawn carts of fruit and lumber—even the occasional cow ambling along, ignoring the blare of honking horns. Trash is strewn about, and the landscape is dotted with aluminum shacks.

In stark contrast to the chaotic street scene are numerous cybercafes and neonlit pubs, modern outposts filled with young software engineers unwinding over Kingfisher beer. Once known as a "garden city" and a "pensioner's paradise" for its greenery and temperate climate, Bangalore has become the Silicon Valley of India, home to leading outsourcing companies, like Wipro and Infosys Technologies, and many Western corporations, including General Electric and Philips Electronics.

The sprawling corporate campuses of India's third-party vendors are replete with tennis courts, golf carts for transportation, swimming pools, open-air cafeterias, waterfalls, palm trees, smoking areas, training centers, health clubs, polished granite lobbies and videoconferencing facilities. The juxtaposition of these corporate headquarters and their surrounding areas is so stark that Indians refer to the business campuses as "islands."

Summing up the contrast, Raman Roy, president of Wipro Spectramind, India's leading provider of outsourced business processes, notes: "The common impression of India is of people going to work on a bullock cart while they talk on their cell phone."

Chief Executive (U.S.), May 2004, i198, p28(4).

© 2004 Chief Executive Publishing.

That picture has stirred a roiling debate over just how many more jobs India—arguably the world's current outsourcing capital—can absorb in the realms of both business process and information technology. On one side of the debate, skeptics argue that India's ancient and sagging infrastructure places an inherent limit on how many jobs can move here. On the other side, optimists believe the vast numbers of educated, skilled and willing workers means India can absorb hundreds of thousands of more jobs.

To be sure, the recent growth of India's outsourcing sector, now worth $12 billion a year in sales, has been nothing short of spectacular. The four-year-old business process outsourcing (BPO) segment, made up of customer-service call centers and administrative facilities handling airline reservations, mortgage applications and insurance claims, is projected to grow by 54 percent this year, to $3.6 billion, on top of a 59-percent growth rate last year, according to the National Association of Software and Service Companies (NASSCOM). The more than decade-old information technology services and products industry is forecast to increase 17 percent, to $8.4 billion, after an 18-percent jump the year before, according to NASSCOM, which estimates the number of IT professionals in India at 650,000, up dramatically from 6,800 in 1985. By 2008, the Indian outsourcing market will reach $77 billion, with 2 million employees, up from 770,000 currently, predicts McKinsey & Co.

But there are numerous threats to India's continued dominance in outsourcing. While telecommunications have improved considerably with cell phones, satellite transmissions and transoceanic fiber optic cable, most other utilities and services have not been updated. Electric power is so unreliable that Wipro Spectramind and other corporations have backup generators. "We are lucky to get 15 hours of electricity daily from the government," says Roy. Many firms have their own water supply, too.

A new highway under construction, called the Golden Quadrilateral and linking Mumbai, New Delhi, Chennai, Kolkata and other Indian cities, won't be completed for a couple of years. It takes an hour to travel 20 kilometers (12 miles) on Bangalore's congested roads to reach the city's outsourcing hubs in Electronics City and Whitefield. Construction of a new international airport to open up more direct flights to Bangalore from cities in Europe and the U.S. hasn't begun. Hotel reservations at the luxurious Taj West End and the trendy Leela Palace are hard to get, and few new hotels are being built. While there has been much talk about an elevated railway for Bangalore, so far it's only talk. And with no mass transit option yet, most corporations have to bus their employees to and from work.

AN EDGE ON CHINA

Aside from India's poor infrastructure, there is international competition, a dearth of workers with managerial skills to fill mid-level jobs and turnover rates of as high as 50 percent among entry-level workers in the back-office services industry. In terms of emerging competitors for outsourcing business, China is an IT stronghold, the Philippines is a base for bilingual Spanish-English language skill and Eastern Europe is a customer service center for Europe. Even Wipro Spectramind, a subsidiary of Wipro, is going abroad, adding a 200-person development center in Shanghai and a Czech Republic branch to handle European customers.

In an analysis of outsourcing locations, the Gartner Group ranks India ahead of China in language skills, government support, labor pool, costs, educational system, cultural compatibility and data/IP security. The only areas where China outperforms India are infrastructure and political stability. "China has made tremendous progress, and for India to fulfill its potential it needs to work on new roads, hotels, water supply, air transport and mass transit," says Infosys CEO Nandan Nilekani from his informal, working office at the company's sprawling 70-acre headquarters in Electronics City.

So far, managing the sheer speed of growth has been the most challenging part of Nilekani's job. Infosys is eyeing revenues of $1 billion for the fiscal year ending March 2004, up from $753 million the year before and from $121 million in 1999. "When we founded this company, we didn't visualize this kind of dimension—the enormity of what is possible," Nilekani says.

Continued growth in outsourcing business faces another significant hurdle: the political outcry over the loss of U.S. jobs. "A backlash has developed in the run-up to the elections," notes Nilekani, "but frankly we believe the world operates on a free-trade basis and you trade on what you are good at." Ultimately, he says, U.S. companies see improved productivity and stronger financials as a result, and that will lead to increased U.S. exports to Indian companies.

The sentiment among outsourcing leaders is that the political controversy will subside once the elections are over, and that the "noise" is out of proportion to the issue. For instance, Forrester Research estimates that 300,000 U.S. jobs have been lost to outsourcing, out of a total 2.7 million U.S. job losses. Even so, Azim Premji, chairman and managing director at Wipro, says he's keeping a low profile. Hence, he recently turned down a speaking engagement at the Asia Society in New York.

Backlash aside, Premji remains sanguine about India's ability to accommodate more jobs. "Infrastructure? Of course it's a problem," says the CEO from his serene office overlooking the firm's ultramodern headquarters (which outclasses any Silicon Valley or Seattle-area high-tech campus). But he points to rapid telecommunications improvements and a speedup of road, bridge and port construction with government liberalization. Upcoming privatization in the power industry within four years should put the "power issues behind us," adds Premji, who is considered the Bill Gates of India for his fortune in Wipro shares, which are listed on the New York Stock Exchange.

To maintain its growth, India clearly will have to speed up those infrastructure improvements. Bangalore is one of the more modern cities in India, but by comparison, Shanghai—a key rival—looks like it belongs on a futuristic planet, with its mag-lev elevated railway, efficient subway system, new international airport, steady power supplies and well-engineered roads and bridges. Domestic rivalry within India, meanwhile, is keeping the pressure on. Bangalore vies for business with Hyderabad to the South and with the New Delhi suburbs of Noida and Gurgaon to the North. Pune, Chennai and Kolkata are also becoming contenders.

Assuming improvements continue, Premji believes India could easily see outsourcing growth of 20 to 25 percent over the next five years. Wipro saw revenues climb 44 percent, to $343 million, in the third quarter ending December 2003 compared with the same period a year earlier while net income grew 22 percent, to $58 million. Annual figures due to be released shortly are likely to show continued gains. "The opportunity is very huge and mammoth," says Roy of Wipro Spectramind, which Wipro acquired in July 2002 to capitalize on this booming area of outsourcing. Post-acquisition, the Wipro subsidiary has grown to 8,500 employees, up from 2,500, with revenues of $100 million.

MORE ROOM FOR GROWTH

One pleased client among Wipro's 300 customers is Blackwell Book Services, a division of the British bookseller. Two years ago, it hired a small Wipro software group to help supplement its 20-person software team in Portland, Ore. "The quality of the work is very sound," says Cloy Swartzendruber, Blackwell's vice president of IT. "You get exactly what you ask for—and then some," he says. The team in India has specialized skills in working with IBM mainframes that their U.S. counterparts lack, at one-half to one-third the fee of U.S. engineers. Even so, he stresses that no one in the U.S. office has lost their job to the Indian software team, although some work has dropped off with U.S. consulting firms.

There's plenty of room for India's outsourcing sector to attract more customers from abroad. India claims only 2 percent of the $180-billion software-products market worldwide, according to NASSCOM. In BPO, however, India already claims a dominant 80 percent of the global market.

Most booms don't last forever, though, and Gartner Research Vice President Rita Terdiman says Indian outsourcing should reach maturity by 2007. Already, consolidation is occurring. "The big are getting bigger and most clients want to go with one vendor and one brand name," says Nilekani. McKinsey partner Jayant Sinha argues that one or two major global players with lower cost and value-added services will dominate the business.

The single biggest question revolves around labor. India's labor pool stands at 470 million people, with 9 million new entrants each year. Incredibly, Infosys claims to have received 1 million applications last year for 9,000 new jobs. While software programming prowess abounds, managerial experience is thin. "We have to bring managers in from overseas or hire them from other industries," says Akshaya Bhargava, CEO of Progeon, a BPO partnership with Infosys.

Training a steady influx of workers is a big job. Wipro has an on-site "university" with 70 full-time faculty who train 2,500 new yearly recruits for 35 days and teach management skills and software programming courses. Students get reimbursed for the coursework when they pass certification tests.

At call centers, getting inquiries resolved on the first attempt is a key goal. Roy says his firm has seen a 40- to 50-percent improvement in "first-time resolution" over the past year and adds, "eight out of 10 people don't call back."

But high turnover of 50 percent-plus at most centers is a challenge. Causing that turnover are everything from night shifts answering calls from strangers on the other side of the globe, disillusionment with a mundane routine, few opportunities for advancement and higher salary offers from rivals. "We have to position BPO as not just fun, but a long-term career," says Progeon's Bhargava, who adds that industry specialization could be one way to relieve the monotony and offer career advancement.

One fun thing for the workers is learning how to speak English with a British accent, for, say, HSBC, and with an American accent for Delta Air Lines, for example. "The critical things in outsourcing are getting the food served on time, the transport to and from work on time and the matrimonial references," says Tiger Ramesh, head of BPO outsourcing at iGate. Within India's traditional practice of arranged marriages, he explains, the three questions that a prospective matchmaker wants to know about a groom are, Does he work for the organization?, Does he have an opportunity to go the U.S.?, and if so, Will the organization sponsor a Hl-B visa work permit? Those visas cover technology workers.

Multinational companies such as American Express, Standard Chartered and Citigroup also are having to grapple with these issues as their numbers multiply, increasing to 32 percent of the Indian outsourcing market last year, up from 26 percent in 2002.

Dutch electronics company Philips maintains a huge R & D center in Bangalore, with some 1,150 software engineers to design chips for all of Philips DVDs and some other electronic devices. The labs are the biggest among Philips' 25 R & D centers employing 2,000 overall, says Philips Software CEO Bob Hoekstra. The Indian group claims 23 patents and has saved Philips 100 million euros in product development costs since it started seven years ago, says Hoekstra. Salaries are 50 to 70 percent lower than in the U.S. or Europe, and there is no shortage of engineer applicants, he adds. "I could think of 1,000 reasons that we would fail with this offshore operation," says Hoekstra. "But the engineers here have a keen ability to stretch themselves and they have a high level of motivation."

Likewise, Indian CEOs argue that the quality of their labor pool will overcome all the other challenges. "When CEOs come here from abroad and look under the hood, they are absolutely amazed," says Nilekani, looking out over a room filled with fresh-faced software engineers debating the finer points of programming code. "The thing that is winning this for India is the human capital," he adds. If he's right, jobs will keep moving to India—for many years to come.

8

How Nike Figured
Out China

Matthew Forney, with reporting by Daren Fonda and Neil Gough

The China market is finally for real. To the country's new consumers, Western products mean one thing: status. They can't get enough of those Air Jordans.

Nike swung into action even before most Chinese knew they had a new hero. The moment hurdler Liu Xiang became the country's first Olympic medalist in a short-distance speed event—he claimed the gold with a new Olympic record in the 110-m hurdles on Aug. 28—Nike launched a television advertisement in China showing Liu destroying the field and superimposed a series of questions designed to set nationalistic teeth on edge. "Asians lack muscle?" asked one. "Asians lack the will to win?" Then came the kicker, as Liu raised his arms above the trademark Swoosh on his shoulder: "Stereotypes are made to be broken." It was an instant success. "Nike understands why Chinese are proud," says Li Yao, a weekend player at Swoosh-bedecked basketball courts near Beijing's Tiananmen Square.

Such clever marketing tactics have helped make Nike the icon for the new China. According to a recent Hill & Knowlton survey, Chinese consider Nike the Middle Kingdom's "coolest brand." Just as a new Flying Pigeon bicycle defined success when reforms began in the 1980s and a washing machine that could also scrub potatoes became the status symbol a decade later, so the Air Jordan—or any number of Nike products turned out in factories across

Time, Oct 25, 2004, v164, i17, pA8 (TIME Bonus Section November 2004: Global Business/Marketing).

Asia—has become the symbol of success for China's new middle class. Sales rose 66% last year, to an estimated $300 million, and Nike is opening an average of 1.5 new stores a day in China. Yes, a day. The goal is to migrate inland from China's richer east-coast towns in time for the outpouring of interest in sports that will accompany the 2008 Summer Olympics in Beijing. How did Nike build such a booming business? For starters, the company promoted the right sports and launched a series of inspired ad campaigns. But the story of how Nike cracked the China code has as much to do with the rise of China's new middle class, which is hungry for Western gear and individualism, and Nike's ability to tap into that hunger.

Americans have dreamed of penetrating the elusive China market since traders began peddling opium to Chinese addicts in exchange for tea and spices in the 19th century. War and communism conspired to keep the Chinese poor and Westerners out. But with the rise of a newly affluent class and the rapid growth of the country's economy, the China market has become the fastest growing for almost any American company you can think of. Although Washington runs a huge trade deficit with Beijing, exports to China have risen 76% in the past three years. According to a survey by the American Chamber of Commerce, 3 out of 4 U.S. companies say their China operations are profitable; most say their margins are higher in China than elsewhere in the world. "For companies selling consumer items, a presence here is essential," says Jim Gradoville, chairman of the American Chamber in China.

The Chinese government may have a love-hate relationship with the West—eager for Western technology yet threatened by democracy—but for Chinese consumers, Western goods mean one thing: status. Chinese-made Lenovo (formerly Legend) computers used to outsell foreign competitors 2 to 1; now more expensive Dells are closing the gap. Foreign-made refrigerators are displacing Haier as the favorite in China's kitchens. Chinese dress in their baggiest jeans to sit at Starbucks, which has opened 100 outlets and plans hundreds more. China's biggest seller of athletic shoes, Li Ning, recently surrendered its top position to Nike, even though Nike's shoes—upwards of $100 a pair—cost twice as much. The new middle class "seeks Western culture," says Zhang Wanli, a social scientist at the Chinese Academy of Social Sciences. "Nike was smart because it didn't enter China selling usefulness, but selling status."

The quest for cool hooked Zhang Han early. An art student in a loose Donald Duck T shirt and Carhartt work pants, Zhang, 20, has gone from occasional basketball player to All-Star consumer. He pries open his bedroom closet to reveal 19 pairs of Air Jordans, a full line of Dunks and signature shoes of NBA stars like Vince Carter—more than 60 pairs costing $6,000. Zhang began gathering Nikes in the 1990s after a cousin sent some from Japan; his businessman father bankrolls his acquisitions. "Most Chinese can't afford this stuff," Zhang says, "but I know people with hundreds of pairs." Then he climbs into his jeep to drive his girlfriend to McDonald's.

Zhang hadn't yet been born when Nike founder Phil Knight first traveled to China in 1980, before Beijing could even ship to U.S. ports; the country was just emerging from the turmoil of the Cultural Revolution. By the mid-'80s,

Knight had moved much of his production to China from South Korea and Taiwan. But he saw China as more than a workshop. "There are 2 billion feet out there," former Nike executives recall his saying. "Go get them!"

Phase 1, getting the Swoosh recognized, proved relatively easy. Nike outfitted top Chinese athletes and sponsored all the teams in China's new pro basketball league in 1995. But the company had its share of horror stories too, struggling with production problems (gray sneakers instead of white), rampant knock-offs, then criticism that it was exploiting Chinese labor. Cracking the market in a big way seemed impossible. Why would the Chinese consumer spend so much—twice the average monthly salary back in the late 1990s—on a pair of sneakers?

Sports simply wasn't a factor in a country where, since the days of Confucius, education levels and test scores dictated success. So Nike executives set themselves a potentially quixotic challenge: to change China's culture. Recalls Terry Rhoads, then director of sports marketing for Nike in China: "We thought, 'We won't get anything if they don't play sports.'" A Chinese speaker, Rhoads saw basketball as Nike's ticket. He donated equipment to Shanghai's high schools and paid them to open their basketball courts to the public after hours. He put together three-on-three tournaments and founded the city's first high school basketball league, the Nike League, which has spread to 17 cities. At games, Rhoads blasted the recorded sound of cheering to encourage strait-laced fans to loosen up, and he arranged for the state-run television network to broadcast the finals nationally. The Chinese responded: sales through the 1990s picked up 60% a year. "Our goal was to hook kids into Nike early and hold them for life," says Rhoads, who now runs a Shanghai-based sports marketing company, Zou Marketing. Nike also hitched its wagon to the NBA (which had begun televising games in China), bringing players like Michael Jordan for visits. Slowly but surely, in-the-know Chinese came to call sneakers "Nai-ke."

And those sneakers brought with them a lot more than just basketball. Nike gambled that the new middle class, now some 40 million people who make an average of $8,500 a year for a family of three, was developing a whole new set of values, centered on individualism. Nike unabashedly made American culture its selling point, with ads that challenge China's traditional, group-oriented ethos. This year the company released Internet teaser clips showing a faceless but Asian-looking high school basketball player shaking-and-baking his way through a defense. It was timed to coincide with Nike tournaments around the country and concluded with the question, "Is this you?" The viral advertisement drew 5 million e-mails. Nike then aired TV spots contrasting Chinese-style team-oriented play with a more individualistic American style, complete with a theme song blending traditional Chinese music and hip-hop.

Starting in 2001, Nike coined a new phrase for its China marketing, borrowing from American black street culture: "Hip Hoop." The idea is to "connect Nike with a creative lifestyle," says Frank Pan, Nike's current director of sports marketing for China. The company's Chinese website even encourages rap-style trash talk. "Shanghai rubbish, you lose again!" reads a typical posting for a Nike League high school game. The hip-hop message "connects the disparate elements of black cool culture and associates it with Nike," says Edward Bell, director of planning for Ogilvy & Mather in Hong Kong. "But black culture can be aggressive, and Nike softens it to make it more acceptable" to Chinese. At a recent store opening in Shanghai, Nike flew in a street-ball team from Beijing. The visitors humiliated their opponents while speakers blasted rapper 50 Cent as he informed the Chinese audience that he is a P-I-M-P with impure designs on their mothers.

Thanks in part to Nike's promotions, urban hip-hop culture is all the rage among young Chinese. One of Beijing's leading DJs, Gu Yu, credits Nike with "making me the person I am." Handsome and tall under a mop of shoulder-length hair, Gu got hooked on hip-hop after hearing rapper Black Rob rhyme praises to Nike in a television ad. Gu learned more on Nike's Internet page and persuaded overseas friends to send him music. Now they send something else too: limited-edition Nikes unavailable in China. Gu and his partner sell them in their shop, Upward, to Beijing's several hundred "sneaker friends" and wear them while spinning tunes in Beijing's top clubs. To them, scoring rare soles and playing banned music are part of the same rebellious experience. "Because of the government, Chinese aren't allowed access to a lot of these things," says Gu's partner, Ji Ming, "but with our shop and Nike-style music, they can get what they want."

The Nike phenomenon is challenging Confucian-style deference to elders too. At the Nike shop in a ritzy Shanghai shopping mall, Zhen Zhiye, 22, a dental hygienist in a miniskirt, persuades her elderly aunt, who has worn only cheap sneakers that she says "make my feet stink," to drop $60 on a new pair. Zhen explains the "fragrant possibilities" of higher-quality shoes and chides her aunt for her dowdy ways. Her aunt settles on a cross trainer. For most of China's history, this exchange would have been unthinkable. "In our tradition, elders pass culture to youth," says researcher Zhang. "Now it's a great reversal, with parents and grandparents eating and clothing themselves like children."

Success aside, Nike has had its stumbles. When it began outfitting Chinese professional soccer teams in the mid-1990s, its ill-fitting cleats caused heel sores so painful that Nike had to let its athletes wear Adidas (with black tape over the trademark). In 1997, Nike ramped up production just before the Asian banking crisis killed demand, then flooded the market with cheap shoes, undercutting its own retailers and driving many into the arms of Adidas. Two years later, the company created a $15 Swoosh-bearing canvas sneaker designed for poor Chinese. The "World Shoe" flopped so badly that Nike killed it.

Yet all that amounts to a frayed shoelace compared with losing China's most famous living human. Yao Ming had worn Nike since Rhoads discovered him as a skinny kid with a sweet jumper—and brought him some size 18s made for NBA All-Star Alonzo Mourning. In 1999 he signed Yao to a four-year contract worth $200,000. But Nike let his contract expire last year. Yao defected to Reebok for an estimated $100 million. The failure leaves Nike executives visibly dejected. "The only thing I know is, we lost Yao Ming," says a Shanghai executive who negotiated with the star.

Nike is determined not to repeat the mistake. It has already signed China's next NBA prospect, the 7-ft. Yi Jianlian, 18, who plays for the Guangdong Tigers. And the company has resolved problems that dogged it a few years ago. Nike has cleaned up its shop floors. It cut its footwear suppliers in China from 40 to 16, and 15 of those sell only to Nike, allowing the company to monitor conditions more easily. At Shoetown in the southern city of Guangzhou, 10,000 mostly female laborers work legal hours stitching shoes for $95 a month—more than minimum wage. "They've made huge progress," says Li Qiang, director of New York City—based China Labor Watch.

In China, Nike is hardly viewed as the ugly imperialist. In fact, the company's celebration of American culture is totally in synch with the Chinese as they hurtle into a chaotic, freer time. In July, at a Nike three-on-three competition in the capital, a Chinese DJ named Jo Eli played songs like I'll Be Damned off his Dell computer. "Nike says play hip-hop because that's what blacks listen to," he says. "The government doesn't exactly promote these things. But we can all expose ourselves to something new." That sounds pretty close to a Chinese translation of "Just Do It."

Buying Power
Annual per capita disposable income of urban Chinese:
'99 $713
'04 $1,174*

*ESTIMATE. SOURCE: National Bureau of Statistics

What's Hip in China

Defining Cool
Young Chinese may know what "cool" is these days, but they had to invent a word for it: ku. Yet just what is ku? Public relations firm Hill & Knowlton decided to find out. What is it? In a recent survey, 1,200 university students in Beijing and Shanghai rated which personality traits define a person as cool. Stodgy socialism is, like so yesterday: Individualistic, innovative 47%

   Stylish 13.5%
   Dynamic, capable 9%
   Easygoing, relaxed 7.5%
   Other/uncategorizable 22.5%

Who has it?
The survey also asked the students to name the world's coolest brands. Nike was way out ahead, and there wasn't a single Chinese brand in the group:

   Nike 30.8%
   Sony 15.9%
   Adidas 15.1%
   BMW 10.1%
   Microsoft 9.0%
   Coca-Cola 8.9%
   IBM 8.2%

SOURCE: Hill & Knowlton

9

All This Progress
Is Killing Us,
Bite by Bite

Gregg Easterbrook

Your great-great grandparents would find it hard to believe the Boeing 747, but perhaps they'd have a harder time believing last week's news that obesity has become the second-leading cause of death in the United States. Too much food a menace instead of too little! A study released by the federal Centers for Disease Control ranked "poor diet and physical inactivity" as the cause of 400,000 United States deaths in 2000, trailing only fatalities from tobacco. Obesity, the C.D.C. said, now kills five times as many Americans as "microbial agents," that is, infectious disease.

Moon landings might seem less shocking to your great-great grandparents than abundance of food causing five times as many deaths as germs; OutKast might seem less bizarre to them than the House passing legislation last week to exempt restaurants from being sued for serving portions that are too large.

Your recent ancestors would further be stunned by the notion of plump poverty. A century ago, the poor were as lean as fence posts; worry about where to get the next meal was a constant companion for millions. Today, America's least well-off are so surrounded by double cheeseburgers, chicken buckets, extra-large pizzas and supersized fries that they are more likely to be overweight than the population as a whole.

The New York Times, March 14, 2004, pWK5(L), col 01, (27 col in).

41

But the expanding waistline is not only a problem of lower-income Americans who dine too often on fast food. Today, the typical American is overweight, according to the C.D.C., which estimates that 64 percent of American citizens are carrying too many pounds for their height. Obesity and sedentary living are rising so fast that their health consequences may soon supplant tobacco as the No. 1 preventable cause of death, the C.D.C. predicts. Rates of heart disease, stroke and many cancers are in decline, while life expectancy is increasing—but ever-rising readings on the bathroom scale may be canceling out what would otherwise be dramatic gains in public health.

O.K., it's hard to be opposed to food. But the epidemic of obesity epitomizes the unsettled character of progress in affluent Western society. Our lives are characterized by too much of a good thing—too much to eat, to buy, to watch and to do, excess at every turn. Sometimes achievement itself engenders the excess: today's agriculture creates so much food at such low cost that who can resist that extra helping?

Consider other examples in which society's success seems to be backfiring on our health or well-being.

PRODUCTIVITY

Higher productivity is essential to rising living standards and to the declining prices of goods and services. But higher productivity may lead to fewer jobs.

Early in the postwar era, analysts fretted that automation would take over manufacturing, throwing everyone out of work. That fear went unrealized for a generation, in part because robots and computers weren't good at much. Today, near-automated manufacturing is becoming a reality. Newly built factories often require only a fraction of the work force of the plants they replace. Office technology, meanwhile, now allows a few to do what once required a whole hive of worker bees.

There may come a point when the gains from higher productivity pale before the job losses. But even if that point does not come, rapid technological change is instilling anxiety about future employment: anxiety that makes it hard to appreciate and enjoy what productivity creates.

TRAFFIC

Cars are much better than they were a few decades ago—more comfortable, powerful and reliable. They are equipped with safety features like air bags and stuffed with CD players, satellite radios and talking navigation gizmos. Adjusted for consumers' rising buying power, the typical powerful new car costs less than one a generation ago.

But in part because cars are so desirable and affordable, roads are increasingly clogged with traffic. Today in the United States, there are 230 million cars and trucks in operation, and only 193 million licensed drivers—more vehicles than drivers! Studies by the Federal Highway Administration show that in the 30 largest cities, total time lost to traffic jams has almost quintupled since 1980.

Worse, prosperity has made possible the popularity of S.U.V.'s and the misnamed "light" pickup trucks, which now account for half of all new-car sales. Exempt from the fuel-economy standards that apply to regular cars, sport utility vehicles and pickup trucks sustain American dependence on Persian Gulf oil. A new study in the *Journal of Risk and Uncertainty* showed that the rise in S.U.V.'s and pickup trucks "leads to substantially more fatalities" on the road.

So just as longevity might be improving at a faster clip were it not for expanding waistlines, death rates in traffic accidents might show a more positive trend were it not for the S.U.V. explosion.

The proliferation of cars also encourages us to drive rather than walk. A century ago, the typical American walked three miles a day; now the average is less than a quarter mile a day. Some research suggests that the sedentary lifestyle, rather than weight itself, is the real threat; a chubby person who is physically active will be O.K. Studies also show that it is not necessary to do aerobics to get the benefits of exercise; a half-hour a day of brisk walking is sufficient. But more cars, driven more miles, mean less walking.

STRESS

It's not just in your mind: Researchers believe stress levels really are rising. People who are overweight or inactive experience more stress than others, and that now applies to the majority. Insufficient sleep increases stress, and Americans now sleep on average only seven hours a night, versus eight hours for our parents' generation and 10 hours for our great-grandparents'.

Research by Bruce McEwen, a neuroendocrinologist at Rockefeller University in New York, suggests that modern stress, in addition to making life unpleasant, can impair immune function—again, canceling out health gains that might otherwise occur.

Prosperity brings many other mixed blessings. Living standards keep rising, but so does incidence of clinical depression. Cellphones are convenient, but make it impossible to escape from office calls. E-mail is cheap and fast, if you don't mind deleting hundreds of spam messages. The Internet and cable television improve communication, but deluge us with the junkiest aspects of culture.

Americans live in ever-nicer, ever-larger houses, but new homes and the businesses that serve them have to go somewhere. Sprawl continues at a maddening pace, while once-rustic areas may now be gridlocked with S.U.V.'s and power boats.

Agricultural yields continue rising, yet that means fewer family farms are needed. Biotechnology may allow us to live longer, but may leave us dependent on costly synthetic drugs. There are many similar examples.

Increasingly, Western life is afflicted by the paradoxes of progress. Material circumstances keep improving, yet our quality of life may be no better as a result—especially in those cases, like food, where enough becomes too much.

"The maximum is not the optimum," the ecologist Garrett Hardin, who died last year, liked to say. Americans are choosing the maximum, and it does not necessarily make us healthier or happier.

10

Indians Go Home, but Don't Leave U.S. Behind

Amy Waldman

Snigdha Dhar sat in the echoing emptiness of her new home, her husband off at work, her 7-year-old son prattling on about Pizza Hut. The weather outside was California balmy. Children rode bicycles on wide smooth streets. Construction workers toiled on more villas like hers—white paint, red roofs, green lawns—and the community center's three pools.

Six years ago, Mrs. Dhar and her husband, Subhash, a vice president at Infosys Technologies, the Indian software giant, migrated like thousands of Indians before them, to America's Silicon Valley and its suburban good life.

But Silicon Valley is not where their gated housing colony, Palm Meadows, sits. Like growing numbers of professional Indians who once saw their only hope for good jobs and good lives in the West, the Dhars have returned home to India.

Drawn by a booming economy, in which outsourcing is playing a crucial role, and the money to buy the lifestyle they had in America, Indians are returning in large numbers, many to this high-technology hub.

What began as a trickle in the late 1990's is now substantial enough to be talked about as a "reverse brain drain." By one estimate, there are 35,000 "returned nonresident Indians" in Bangalore, with many more scattered across India.

The New York Times, July 24, 2004, pA1, col 02, (54 col in).

For this still developing country, the implications of the reverse migration are potentially vast.

For decades, it has watched many of its best-educated move abroad, never to come back. Now a small portion of that talent is returning, their influence amplified beyond their numbers by their high-level skills and education, new cultural perspective and, in many cases, ample wealth. They are both staffing and starting companies, 110 of which set up shop in Bangalore in just the year that ended in March.

In some cases, they are seeking to refashion India implicitly in America's image. It takes leaving and returning, said Arjun Kalyanpur, a radiologist who returned in 1999, to ask, "Why should my country be any less than the country I was in?"

This impulse is not universally welcomed by some Indians who never left and who see a globalized elite—many of whom now carry American passports, not Indian—importing a Western culture as distorting in its way as British colonialism.

Still, returned reformers are already sparking change. Srikanth Nadhamuni, who helped design the Intel Pentium chip, is now applying his formidable skills to designing a software platform that could revolutionize the administration of India's local governments.

Lathika Pai, one of the few women in India's high-technology sector, is trying to bring America's best practices for working mothers to the B2K Corporation, her business-process outsourcing company. Others are trying to encourage schools to teach critical thinking, or force government to be more responsive to citizens.

S. Nagarajan, an entrepreneur, calls it "brain gain." "They have not come back just as they went there," he said.

He came back because he saw in India the business opportunity he once saw in America, where he struck it rich in the 1990's. The call center he and his partners started in Bangalore in 2000 with 20 employees now has 3,600, and $30 million in annual revenues.

Others have been drawn back by the tug of family and the almost atavistic pull of roots, or pushed by diminishing job opportunities in Silicon Valley and tightening Americans visa regulations.

Many of them are returning to communities like Palm Meadows, whose developer, the Adarsh Group, advertises "beautiful homes for beautiful people." The liberalization of India's state-run economy over the last 13 years has spawned a suburban culture of luxury housing developments, malls and sport utility vehicles that is also enabling India to compete for its Americanized best and brightest.

"It is amazing what you can get in terms of quality of life," Subhash Dhar said of the India to which he and his family returned about two months ago.

TRYING TO RECONNECT

The little girls wore dresses of rich blues and hot pinks and deep reds. Their ankle bells tinkled as their feet smacked the floor. They cocked their heads and bent their hands up, trying to perfect the poses of a 1,600-year-old Indian dance form, Bharathanatyam, in the community center of a housing complex that bore almost no trace of India.

All the girls were daughters of returnees, like Prasad Kamisetty, an Intel employee back after 15 years, whose sonorous singing accompanied the dancers, and Sunita Maheshwari, a pediatric cardiologist, who kept one eye on the dance lessons and one on her 4-year-old son in the pool outside. They live in a pastel, pastoral gated compound, Regent Place, where two-story houses with barbecues in the backyard line a tree-shaded main lane.

Where Indian parents have long worried about how to give their children sufficient exposure to the English language and Western culture, many returnees say they worry more about how to connect their children to India.

The returnees describe identities in flux, riddled with continuing questions about what to cook, what holidays to celebrate, what languages to speak, and how to interact with a country that sometimes seems as foreign as the United States once did.

Many spent formative years abroad. On their return, they rejoin an upper middle-class tributary of Indian life that represents a mere sliver of this nation's more than a billion people, 300 million of whom remain abjectly poor.

Their communities are secure and closed off, immune from the water shortages and power cuts that plague this city of 6.5 million people. Their children attend private schools, often Western-flavored "international" ones. For lunch, their children want what they ate in America: peanut butter and jelly and potato chips—all now available here.

Dr. Maheshwari and her husband, Arjun Kalyanpur, see the dance class as a way to graft Indian culture onto their daughter Alisha. The private school they have selected is another, where the children squat, Indian-style, at desks on the floor and learn yoga and Hindu traditional hymns.

"We're sort of crosscultural byproducts who are straddling both worlds without necessarily being firmly entrenched in the Indian culture," said Dr. Maheshwari, 38, who is half-American but was raised in India.

The couple came back after eight years away to be closer to their parents, and because she felt she could contribute more in India. She is one of only about 14 pediatric cardiologists in the entire country. In one outpatient clinic, she sees more untreated medical problems than she ever saw at Yale-New Haven Hospital, where she and her husband trained and worked.

Her husband has found himself on the cutting edge of medical outsourcing. A radiologist, Dr. Kalyanpur had resigned himself to a significant pay drop upon his return. Then he proved to Yale that he could accurately read CT scans and other images transmitted via broadband to India. He began working for them from afar before starting his own business, Teleradiology Solutions Inc., in 2002.

He spends his days reading images for the emergency room nightshifts of about 40 American hospitals, compensating for the shortfall of nighttime radiologists in the United States, and being compensated at near-American salary levels. His partner, like him, is American-trained; at least two more Indian-born radiologists are moving back from the United States to work with them.

"India always suffered from the cream of its medical community migrating overseas," he said. "Now there is the possibility to go back."

India changed in the time Dr. Kalyanpur, 39, was away. Where it once took a year to get a phone connection, it may now take a day.

But he changed as well. He and his wife gravitated to Bangalore, where neither of them had ever lived, in part for the cosmopolitanism in its pubs and cultural life. Regent Place drew them because many European expatriates also live there.

"It makes the transition easier," he said.

On his return, India's poverty loomed up at him, and he and his wife grapple with how to deal with it. They raised money to put a playground in the government school in the village across from their housing complex, and are doing the same for another school nearby.

It is a small attempt to bridge India's great and growing gulf. On a Saturday, children with want visible in thin faces, in bare feet and tattered uniforms, scaled the swing set bought by the returnees, whose own children played across the street inside Regent Place.

NEW OUTLETS FOR NEW TALENTS

On a Sunday morning, Ramesh Ramanathan stood before some 40 middle-class Indians in a garden green with banana, coconut, and hibiscus trees.

"How many of us think India is a great country?" he asked the group, all residents of the Pillana Gardens neighborhood.

All hands rose.

"How many of us think India has a great government?"

All hands fell.

"Give a few hours each week to making governance better," he implored the skeptics before him.

Mr. Ramanathan, 40, was at ease, yet somehow stood apart. Was it the jeans and rolled-up shirt sleeves? The hip, slightly floppy haircut? Or his insistence that change was possible in India, when many of those present confessed they had given up?

"We will try our best," one man said in answer to his exhortation.

"'Try' is not good enough," Mr. Ramanathan said.

By the traditional career arcs of the West, or India for that matter, Mr. Ramanathan and his wife, Swathi, did not seem destined for proselytizing for civic activism.

Like many young, ambitious, middle-class Indian couples, they moved to the United States in the 1980's. He earned an M.B.A. from Yale and rose to become a senior executive at Citibank. She earned a master's degree in design from Pratt and became a successful designer. They moved to London, where he ran a $100 million business in corporate derivatives for Citibank.

Among their pastimes, usually with fellow expatriates, was bemoaning their homeland with sentences that began: "The problem with India is." They would ponder why they so easily went forth and succeeded, while back home, India and so many of its people could not.

At the end of 1998, they came back, wanting their children to get to know their grandparents. They have since put their skills and their experience in the West toward improving public governance and working with the urban poor. Mr. Ramanathan made himself an expert in public finance, and spent two years reforming Bangalore's chaotic financial management system, now ranked among the world's best.

In December 2001, they started Janaagraha, a civic movement intended to make citizens demand greater accountability and effectiveness from their government. The monthly review meetings in municipal wards also help bind the middle class and poo—to build a community, in short, strong enough to challenge a government imbued with both colonial and socialist assumptions that it knows better than the people.

"In America, citizens have reluctantly let government into their lives," he said. "Here government is reluctantly letting citizens in." As part of what he calls the "lucky generation" that has been able to succeed abroad, he said, "If we don't come back and say there is an alternative, who is going to do it?"

He and other returnees believe that India remains too reliant on personal relationships, decisions and whims, and they have resolved to build American-style systems.

That is the focus of Srikanth Nadhamuni, who returned two years ago after 16 years in America, most of it spent in Silicon Valley, where he helped to develop the Sun Microsystems Ultrasparc and Intel Pentium chips.

When he returned, he was appalled by Bangalore's pollution, traffic and poor roads. Tax revenues were not growing commensurate with cities, and therefore neither were basic services. Wealthy individuals and companies had swanky homes and offices, but they were islands.

In response, he began developing an "e-government" software platform that uses digital mapping to permit far more accurate property tax assessments and collection. It will allow for electronic tax payment, birth and death registrations, the filing of citizen grievances, the public tracking of small infrastructure projects, and more.

In Bangalore, the system has already brought in hundreds of thousands of dollars in additional property tax revenue and has reduced corruption. The

Delhi Municipal Corporation—the world's second-largest municipality after Tokyo—will test it soon.

Mr. Nadhamuni wants others, especially in information technology, to offer their talents to India. "We are making a couple of billion dollars of software exports, but we are not solving India's problems," he said. "We are solving the world's problems." He says his mission is "even better than being on the Pentium project."

His work abroad, like Mr. Ramanathan's, has made it possible to be a full-time volunteer, living off savings potentially for life by taking advantage of the much lower cost of living. In Bangalore, Mr. Nadhamuni said, he can live well on $1,500 a month.

"This is not to prove a point that we're back here," he said. "We've gotten used to the U.S. If I have a huge drop in my standard of living, I'm not going to be effective."

On a Saturday morning, his 4-year-old daughter played on the computer in their airy apartment at a gated apartment complex, the Golden Enclave.

"Build a fortress like Tipu Sultan's fortress," Mr. Nadhamuni said, trying to entice her to the wooden blocks on the floor with a reference to the 18th-century warrior who challenged the British colonial rulers. "Sim City," she clamored, her preference clearly for the American-designed computer game in which you alone shape the virtual urban landscape on the screen.

11

A Cultural Grand Salaam: Can 2 Billion People Be Wrong?

Richard Corliss, with Simon Crittle, Lina Lofaro, Jyoti Thottam, Desa Philadelphia, and David Thigpen

The music, movies, and literature of South Asia are the most popular in the world. Now America is falling under their spell.

The brash young man seizes the stage of Manhattan's Broadway Theater, sings and dances to a vigorous bhangra and, feeling his rock-star-in-the-making oats, shouts, "Are ya with me, Bombay?... Are ya with me, New York." This scene from the new musical *Bombay Dreams* poses the cultural question of the moment. South Asian pop—Bollywood movies, Indian music and dance, the whole vibrant masala of subcontinental culture—not only enthralls a billion Indians at home but also spans half the world, from Africa and the Middle East to Eastern Europe and the Indian diaspora in Britain and the U.S. Now Indi-pop is close to a critical mass in the U.S. The 2 million American Desis (mainly people of Indian and Pakistani heritage) have made it a burgeoning niche industry. But can it finally catch on in the mall theaters and dance clubs and living rooms of America? Will ya be with it, New York? New Orleans? Nebraska?

Time, May 3, 2004, v163, i18, p64.

The cultural stew is simmering and ready to boil over. Just as Indian food graduated from big-city exotica to mainstream international cuisine, Indi-pop culture could become a new part of American pop culture. It certainly has the energy and glamour to curry favor with more than those who favor curry. It might even gain the hipness it has in Britain—where, as Meera Syal, the original librettist of Bombay Dreams, boldly said, "Brown is the new black."

This process, notes writer Hanif Kureishi, "is inevitable, because culture moves forward by taking new and original voices from the margin and moving them into the center. You saw it with Elvis. You saw it with Toni Morrison." If *Bombay Dreams* is a hit, you may see it with Indian composer A.R. Rahman. You can already see it in the critical and commercial success of novelists like Kureishi, Jhumpa Lahiri, Michael Ondaatje and Arundhati Roy. Their success has led the way for a slew of South Asians, including Michelle de Kretser (from Sri Lanka), Monica Ali (from Bangladesh) and Mohsin Hamid (from Pakistan).

One of the most fertile areas for East-West cross-pollinations is music. At S.O.B.'s in New York City, Rekha Malhotra, a.k.a. DJ Rekha, plays bhangra, a cool fusion of electronic dance and hip-hop beats with traditional Indian folk sounds. So popular is Rekha, 33, that her parties have become tourist attractions. "I can go anywhere in the country," she says, "and someone will go, 'Oh, I've been to Basement Bhangra.'" At Sonotheque in Chicago, Brian Keigher, 31, spins a popular fusion style known as "Asian underground"— fast, irresistibly danceable music studded with sitars and thumping tablas. Wade your way through the crush on the dance floor, and you will find Indian students, Pakistani locals from Devon Avenue, white clubgoers from the North Side and West Side blacks, always hungry for a new sound. At music clubs and universities, crowds can listen to Funkadesi, a band that mixes Indian music with reggae and funk.

From the dance floor, Indian music percolates to the recording studio. Hip-hopper Jay-Z and British-based Indian producer Panjabi MC served up Beware of the Boys, which featured Jay-Z rapping over a remixed version of a song that Panjabi had made a hit in Britain and India. Even Britney Spears is getting her Ganges on; she used British-South Asian producer Rishi Rich on her last album. And you know a culture is hip when it generates a superhero; that's Bombaby, a cult comic-book out of California.

Then there's Bollywood—Hollywood in Bombay and, by extension, all the country's dozen separate film industries—producing the Indian musicals that nearly everyone in America has heard of and practically no one in America has seen. Bollywood films provide the primary entertainment for half the globe; the top films earn millions more in U.S. theaters catering to Desi audiences. But Bollywood has not dented the mass, or even the class, movie public. The Oscar-nominated *Lagaan* took in 10 times as much in the Desi houses as it did when Sony Pictures Classics gave it a general release. Bollywood films are also hard to find in video stores, although they're easily available online and in Indian-American neighborhoods.

Why are the films having more trouble finding an audience than the music and books? America's current cultural insularity aside, the musicals are a hard sell. At three hours-plus, with family-loyalty plots out of the hoariest Hollywood weepies, and all that singing, a Bollywood epic is too old-fashioned for the art-house crowd and too sedate, too girlie, for young males.

All of which makes *Bombay Dreams* a big risk for Broadway: a $14 million musical with no stars, a score by a composer famous in most of the world (see box, at the end) but not in the U.S., and a story set in the Bollywood milieu unknown to Broadway's conservative audience. Producer Andrew Lloyd Webber hired writer Thomas Meehan (*The Producers, Hairspray*) to cut a lot of in-jokes, pump up the mother love—domesticate the Bollywood beast. Will the transplant work? The show has a $6 million advance; and at a preview last week, the audience, perhaps 25% South Asian, seemed to love the infectious songs and rain-drenched dancing. So salaam, Bombay.

But *Bombay Dreams* needs to fill only 14,000 seats a week. How do you get millions to see an Indian movie? For a true crossover, you need a movie that just happens to be Indian, that pours a familiar tale into an Indian milieu. That's *Marigold,* the story of an American starlet, stranded in India, who works in a Bombay movie to get airfare home and falls for her Indian leading man. Bollywood is not the genre here; it's just the backdrop for a fish-out-of-water plot. Says Steve Gilula of Fox Searchlight, which distributed the breakout hit *Bend It Like Beckham:* "American popular culture is good at absorbing influences from around the world. But we embrace the elements, not the complete form. We have borrowed from parts of the culture and integrated it into ours."

Beckham, Gurinder Chadha's inspirational comedy about a young woman (Parminder Nagra) who flouts her traditional Sikh family values to achieve soccer stardom, is the model for this transcultural form. The film, made for about $6 million, earned $32.5 million in North American theaters and an additional $44 million abroad. It has also given Chadha a chance to try making the first crossover Bollywood-style musical: *Bride and Prejudice,* with Jane Austen's Bennet family transformed into Anglo-Indians and Bollywood goddess Aishwarya Rai in the lead. "It's got the love story, it's got the songs, it's fun—like a Grease," rhapsodizes Rick Sands, COO of Miramax Films, which will distribute *Bride* in the U.S. "It's a Bollywood musical, but it's not going to be 3 1/2 hours long." Chadha, who says, "I don't make Bollywood films, I make British films," calls Bride "a Bollywood-inspired movie for a Western audience."

Beckham had another perk: it landed Nagra a continuing role on *ER.* (Finally! An Indian doctor on a U.S. hospital show.) But while contestants on *The Bachelor* go on a Bollywood-theme date this week, few South Asians are on the big or small screen in the U.S. (*The Simpsons'* Apu doesn't count.)

For the most part, Indians are more successful behind the camera than in front of it. M. Night Shyamalan made the megahits *The Sixth Sense* and *Signs.* Mira Nair, director of *Salaam Bombay* and *Monsoon Wedding,* is making an Indian-infused take on *Vanity Fair,* with Reese Witherspoon as Becky Sharp.

And Nair has a three-film slate for her company, International Bhenji Brigade, financed by an Indian businessman.

"I came from India to Harvard in 1976," Nair recalls, "and I was one of only three Indians in the undergraduate class. Five years ago, when I went back, Harvard had 1,500 South Asian students. Which means in five more years, America will be run by people who look like us. We bear no illusions about the elite anymore. We are the elite."

Now the question is whether the nation's wealthiest minority can have the same impact on show business as it has in business, medicine and technology. And whether 290 million other Americans will want to see them onscreen, dance to their music, go to their shows. About 500 years ago, Columbus sought India and found America. Now it's time for America's cultural consumers to discover India.

That's Desi, As in Desirable

For those who haven't yet tested any Indian treats beyond cumin, tandoori and *Bend It Like Beckham,* here's a primer on some recent works worth exploring. (The DVDs are easiest to find online.)

Books

The Impressionist: Hari Kunzru's satire of the Raj

The Hamilton Case: Michelle de Kretser's novel of colonial Ceylon

Family Matters: Rohinton Mistry's domestic drama in '90s Bombay

DVDs

Maqbool: A Bombay Macbeth; this thug opera owes as much to Scarface as to Shakespeare

Devdas: Soulful suffering in one of the most visually ravishing films ever made

A Peck on the Cheek: Mani Ratnam's blend of tragedy and hope

12

American Icon: Big, Bad S.U.V.'s Are Spreading to Europe

Sarah Lyall

The Land Rover barreled around the narrow corner like a whale splashing into a swimming pool, parking, for lack of a better alternative, in the middle of the road. Needless to say, it was not making many friends.

"I'm totally against those cars," said Giorgio Carpanese, a 48-year-old office worker, gesturing toward the offending vehicle, whose owner could be seen blithely disappearing into a fancy wicker-furniture store. "They're too big; they pollute; they're too expensive. And I think that it's only arrogant people who drive them."

S.U.V.'s, or soovs, as they are called here, are becoming increasingly popular on Rome's traffic-clogged streets, as they are across Europe. But even as more people are attracted by their heft and machismo, a countermovement is developing of those who believe that S.U.V.'s are not only pollution-spewing monstrosities, but also unwieldy symbols of American-style excess.

"They're status markers because they're big and expensive and profligate with the earth's resources," said Steven Stradling, professor of transport psychology at the Transport Research Institute at Napier University in Edinburgh. "There's also a degree of anti-American feeling in Europe, and they are identified as American. They are a symbol of power without responsibility, and that's what we feel about you guys right now."

In the United States, S.U.V.'s are no longer novelties, but until recently they had not made much impact in Europe, the land of ancient, narrow streets and $5-a-gallon gas.

Lately, however, S.U.V. sales have soared, touching off bitter complaints about American cultural imperialism and a flurry of proposed anti-S.U.V. legislation in several countries. So far, though, none of those proposals have passed, and, just as they did in America, S.U.V.'s are spreading steadily across the European landscape.

European wariness of S.U.V.'s is expressed in different ways. In Rome, the city government has proposed charging S.U.V. owners triple the regular rate for permits to drive in the historic city center, a 1.8-square-mile area of narrow streets that is home to 22,000 people. With 50,000 cars and trucks, 300,000 motorbikes and some 600,000 to 700,000 pedestrians using the zone each day, the feeling goes, there is just no room for the unwieldy and intimidating S.U.V.'s.

The city's transportation commissioner, Mario Di Carlo, said that if he could, he would put up signs saying, "Please don't come here with these cars."

"I don't want to be like Freud, but S.U.V.'s are a projection, a compensating thing," Mr. Di Carlo said in an interview. "They're when you want to show how rich, how powerful, how tall, how big you are."

It has proved hard to enact anti-S.U.V. legislation, partly because of the different ways of defining what exactly constitutes an S.U.V., and partly because of the influence of the automobile industry in places like Britain, Germany and Sweden. But that has not stopped leftist politicians from bad-mouthing the cars at every opportunity.

"S.U.V. drivers are less respectful of other people—you can tell by the way they drive," Mr. Di Carlo said. "They park on the sidewalks. Mobility is freedom, but these cars in cities mean immobility, and someone has to have the guts to say it."

The automobile industry, though, says the government is unfairly singling out S.U.V.'s when other cars are just as guilty.

"If they are thinking about passing a new law to protect the environment or avoid pollution in the cities, it should be a serious one, not just something that is going to affect 2 percent to 5 percent of the cars in Italy," said Wanni Zarpellon, general secretary of the Italian Federation of Off-Road Vehicles.

In London, where S.U.V.'s are known derisively as "Chelsea tractors," after an upscale neighborhood in which they are especially thick on the road, Mayor Ken Livingston recently dismissed their drivers as "complete idiots." Drivers report having rude things shouted at them by pedestrians, and a group called the Alliance Against Urban 4x4's has taken to slapping fake tickets on parked S.U.V.'s, citing them for poor vehicle choice in an echo of similar campaigns in the United States.

"People who see Hummers driving around think, 'Oh, disgusting Americans,'" said Sian Berry, a founding member of the group. "We're saying that what happened in America must not be allowed to happen here."

Among other things, she said, her group would like to ban advertising that promotes the inappropriate use of S.U.V.'s, as in a television commercial she saw recently where a man drives up a mountain to fetch an ice cube. "It's saying, 'Please use this car for a really stupid errand,'" Ms. Berry said.

Like the Italian government, the French government has proposed increasing taxes on cars that use more fuel and thus contribute more to global warming, including S.U.V.'s. In Paris, where some members of the city council tried unsuccessfully to ban the cars from the city center during peak traffic times, the council passed a resolution last summer criticizing the cars for their carbon dioxide emissions and their low fuel efficiency, and Deputy Mayor Denis Baupin, a Green Party member, publicly ridiculed the S.U.V. as "a caricature of a car."

In Stockholm, legislators on the left have been pushing the government to levy higher taxes on the cars. But Volvo—which makes the XC90, a popular S.U.V.—is based there, and so far the government has balked.

Understandably, manufacturers of S.U.V.'s are not happy about their poor image in Europe. Among other things, they point out, European-manufactured S.U.V.'s are in many instances more compact and environmentally friendly than their counterparts in the United States, blurring the distinction between different classifications of car and muddying the legislative debate.

"A lot of the criticism comes from envy," said Nigel Wonnacott, a spokesman for the Society of Motor Manufacturers and Traders, which represents the British automobile industry. "If you start stripping down the facts, you learn that S.U.V.'s are not really that much larger than other cars."

"As far as carbon dioxide emissions go, they're not worse than a large executive-class car," he continued. "Where do we go from there—do we start banning those cars, too?"

S.U.V.'s still make up a tiny percentage of the market, but sales have been growing more or less steadily in the last decade. In 1999, 85,247 cars fitting the loose definition of S.U.V.'s were sold in Italy; last year the figure was 108,457 in Italy, according to Jaro Dynamics, which provides market intelligence on the automobile industry. In that time, British sales rose to 159,032 from 98,929, Jaro said.

S.U.V. owners like them for all the familiar reasons. They like their muscularity, their swagger. They feel safe and powerful up there, looking down at everyone else. And although they will probably not say it in so many words, they cannot be unaware of what their S.U.V. says about them: namely, that "they have a lot of money and want to show off," as Marcello Signorile, a Roman taxi driver, put it.

In Rome, it is hard to find anyone who will admit to being an S.U.V. fan, except for the actual owners. One of them, 34-year-old Ivano Stephanelli made no apologies for his impressive gray BMW X5, parked—if jutting out halfway into the street can be considered parked—in front of the pizzeria he owns. "This is a family car, not an ostentatious kind of car."

Mr. Stephanelli, who said the car was perfect for ferrying around his two children, delivering supplies to his restaurant, and tooling up to the family place in Tuscany, argued that he had actually used restraint in selecting it. "My friend got an even bigger car, a Toyota Land Cruiser," he said, "but I'm happy with this one."

His father-in-law, Otto Rino, pronounced the BMW, for which his son-in-law paid 76,000 euros, or about $98,000, with accessories, "awesome" and attributed the mean looks it sometimes attracted to the fact that "other people are jealous."

Not that he spends much time behind the wheel, himself.

"I'm afraid to drive it," he said.

13

Using a New Language in Africa to Save Dying Ones

Marc Lacey

Using the computer in Swahili

Swahili speakers wishing to use a "kompyuta" as computer is rendered in Swahili—have been out of luck when it comes to communicating in their tongue. Computers, no matter how bulky their hard drives or sophisticated their software packages, have not yet mastered Swahili or hundreds of other indigenous African languages.

But that may soon change. Across the continent, linguists are working with experts in information technology to make computers more accessible to Africans who happen not to know English, French or the other major languages that have been programmed into the world's desktops.

There are economic reasons for the outreach. Microsoft, which is working to incorporate Swahili into Microsoft Windows, Microsoft Office and other popular programs, sees a market for its software among the roughly 100 million Swahili speakers in East Africa. The same goes for Google, which last month launched www.google.co.ke, offering a Kenyan version in Swahili of the popular search engine.

But the campaign to Africanize cyberspace is not all about the bottom line. There are hundreds of languages in Africa—some spoken only by a few dozen elders—and they are dying out at an alarming rate. The continent's linguists see the computer as one important way of saving them. Unesco estimates that 90 percent of the world's 6,000 languages are not represented on the Internet, and that one language is disappearing somewhere around the world every two weeks.

"Technology can overrun these languages and entrench Anglophone imperialism," said Tunde Adegbola, a Nigerian computer scientist and linguist who is working to preserve Yoruba, a West African language spoken by millions of people in western Nigeria as well as in Cameroon and Niger. "But if we act, we can use technology to preserve these so-called minority languages."

Experts say that putting local languages on the screen will also lure more Africans to information technology, narrowing the digital divide between the world's rich and poor.

As it is now, Internet cafes are becoming more and more common in even the smallest of African towns, but most of the people at the keyboards are the educated elite. Wireless computer networks are appearing—there is one at the Nairobi airport and another at the Intercontinental Hotel in Kigali, Rwanda's capital—but they are geared for the wealthy not the working class.

Extending the computer era to the remote reaches of Africa requires more than just wiring the villages. Experts say that software must be developed and computer keyboards adapted so that Swahili speakers and those who communicate in Amharic, Yoruba, Hausa, Sesotho and many other languages spoken in Africa feel at home.

Mr. Adegbola, executive director of the African Languages Technology Initiative, has developed a keyboard able to deal with the complexities of Yoruba, a tonal language. Different Yoruba words are written the same way using the Latin alphabet—the tones that differentiate them are indicated by extra punctuation. It can take many different keystrokes to complete a Yoruba word.

To accomplish the same result with fewer, more comfortable keystrokes, Mr. Adegbola made a keyboard without the letters Q, Z, X, C and V, which Yoruba does not use. He repositioned the vowels, which are high-frequency, to more prominent spots and added accent marks and other symbols, creating what he calls Africa's first indigenous language keyboard. Now, Mr. Adegbola is at work on voice recognition software that can convert spoken Yoruba into text.

Related research is under way in Ethiopia. Amharic, the official language, has 345 letters and letter variations, which has made developing a coherent keyboard difficult. Further complicating the project, the country also has its own system of time and its own calendar.

Still, computer experts at Addis Ababa University are making headway. Recently, they came up with a system that will allow Amharic speakers to send text messages, a relatively new phenomenon in the country.

The researchers involved in the project envision it as more than a way for Amharic-speaking teenagers to gossip among themselves. Text messaging could be a development tool, they say, if farmers in remote areas of the country can get instant access to coffee prices or weather reports.

The Ethiopian researchers hope a cellphone maker will see the country's millions of Amharic speakers as a big enough market to turn their concept into a commercial Amharic handset.

Mr. Adegbola has similar dreams. He is distributing his keyboard free to influential Yoruba speakers, hoping to attract some deep-pocketed entrepreneur who could turn it into a business venture.

In South Africa, researchers at the Unit for Language Facilitation and Empowerment at the University of the Free State are working on a computerized translation system between English and two local languages, Afrikaans and Southern Sotho. Cobus Snyman, who heads the project, said the goal is to extend the system to Xhosa, Venda, Tsonga and other South African languages.

One of Microsoft's motivations in localizing its software is to try to head off the movement toward open-source operating systems like Linux, which are increasingly popular. South Africa has already adopted Linux, which it considers more cost efficient and more likely to stimulate local software development.

Patrick Opiyo, the Microsoft official in charge of the Swahili program, portrays the effort as more about community outreach than business development. Besides Swahili, the company is looking at making its products more available to those who speak Amharic, Zulu and Yoruba and the other two widely used languages in Nigeria—Hausa and Igbo.

In Kenya, Microsoft has rounded up some of the region's top Swahili scholars to come up with a glossary of 3,000 technical terms—the first step in the company's effort to make Microsoft products accessible to Swahili speakers.

Sitting around a conference table recently in Microsoft's sleek offices in downtown Nairobi, the linguists discussed how to convey basic words from the computer age in Swahili, also known as Kiswahili, beginning with the most basic one of all.

"When these modern machines arrived, Kiswahili came up with a quick word for something that didn't exist in our culture," said Clara Momanyi, a Swahili professor at Kenyatta University in Nairobi. "That was 'kompyuta.'"

But scholars subsequently opted for a more local term to describe these amazing machines, she said. It is tarakilishi, which is a combination of the word for "image" and the word for "represent."

The Swahili experts grappled with a variety of other words. How does one say folder? Should it be folda, which is commonly used, or kifuko, a more formal term?

Is a fax a faksi, as the Tanzanians call it, or a kipepesi?

Everyone seemed to agree that an e-mail message was a barua pepe, which means a fast letter. Everyone also seemed to agree that the effort they were engaged in to bring Swahili to cyberspace was long overdue.

"Every continent seems to have a language in the computer, and here we are with nothing," said Mwanashehe Saum Mohammed, a Swahili expert at the United States International University in Nairobi and one of the Microsoft consultants. "This will make Africans feel part of the world community. The fact that the continent is full of poor people doesn't mean we shouldn't be on the world map—or in the computer."

14

The Ultimate Luxury Item
Is Now Made in China

Keith Bradsher

Among the carp ponds, duck farms and moldering plywood huts that have long lined the bank of a Pearl River estuary here, a most incongruous newcomer has appeared: a long, towering shed for building very large luxury yachts, a product that has no market in mainland China.

Lion dancers bobbed and weaved as strings of firecrackers sizzled and boomed on July 3 at the official opening of the yacht factory—an emblem of how China is shifting its sights upmarket. Having mastered the manufacture of many inexpensive goods for mass consumption here and abroad, the country is getting into luxury goods, the kinds coveted by the world's most demanding buyers. China's competitive advantage is that it is doing this at lower cost.

Increasingly expensive brands of shoes, clothing and furniture are being made in this country, mostly for domestic consumption but sometimes for export. BMW has begun assembling some of its latest models in China for sale here, and Mercedes and Cadillac are preparing to do the same.

With yachts, though, China is braving a market where it has little recent experience or demand at home.

The economic boom has certainly created plenty of fortunes big enough to afford yachts. But they have never caught on among rich Chinese, who, unlike the boating set in the West, tend to keep their consumption as inconspicuous as possible. And no wonder, considering how widespread tax evasion and dubious dealings are here: few people want their lifestyles to attract official attention.

"You can gamble away $5 million a night, but don't buy something for $5 million and let people know about it," said Roger Liang, the Hong Kong hotel and real estate developer who is the owner and managing director of Kingship Marine, the company that built and runs the yacht factory here.

Besides, China is no one's idea of a yacht-friendly place. The country imposes tight restrictions on pleasure boating along its seacoast, because of concerns regarding Taiwan, and on its rivers, because of heavy barge traffic. That leaves most boaters confined to lakes inland, which are mostly too small and shallow for large powerboats.

Mechanics who are able to repair modern boat engines are scarce. And, in a country once known for its graceful sail-powered junks, so few people now have even a rudimentary knowledge of sailing that selling sailboats in China would be a hopeless exercise, several boating executives said.

Mr. Liang predicted that it would be 10 years before there would be a market in China for the 33-meter (108-foot) yachts that Kingship is building to order in Zhongshan. And it could be even longer before there is a domestic market for a 75-meter (246-foot) yacht like the one that the company is negotiating to build for a foreign buyer.

So, like Cheoy Lee Shipyards of Hong Kong, which owns a shipyard a few miles downstream in Zhuhai that makes mostly commercial vessels but also the occasional pleasure craft, Kingship Marine is angling for export sales.

Its first yacht has already been sold to a European buyer, said Dennis Yong, the sales and marketing director, and the company is close to a deal for a second. Both yachts were started last fall and now stand half-finished in the boatyard, their red steel hulls and dull gray aluminum cabins still in need of outfitting and paint.

Kingship is trying to sell on price, undercutting the Italian, Dutch and American shipbuilders that dominate the luxury boat trade.

"What would normally be a $10 million boat is $7 million," said Dean Leigh-Smith, executive manager of the Gold Coast City Marina near Brisbane, Australia. The saving, he said, is "a lot of money in anyone's language."

Mr. Leigh-Smith's marina, one of the largest in the Southern Hemisphere, has 20 to 25 potential customers for Kingship yachts lined up. The marina has already sold 15 smaller boats—of 40 to 60 feet—made in China, at a Shanghai boatyard, and found the quality generally acceptable despite some initial problems with curtains, carpets, cleats and handrails.

"We've had our small dramas with them, quality control," Mr. Leigh-Smith said. But, he added, "Every time we've gone to the factory and said 'we're not happy with this,' they've rectified it."

As is often the case with manufacturing in China, Kingship is entering the yacht market with a lot of help from abroad.

Mr. Liang is financing and directing the project from Hong Kong. He brought in Mr. Yong from Singapore. Prominent American and Dutch designers drew up the blueprints for Kingship's yachts.

After starting construction of the first yacht with Chinese steel and finding it tough to get plates in the right sizes and shapes, Kingship is assembling the second one from imported steel plates, and plans to do the same with three more. The plates are forged in the Netherlands by Corus, a big European steel maker, and then cut and bent to shape there by Multi Metaal before being shipped here in containers for assembly.

The engines are imported from a Caterpillar factory in Illinois, though two representatives of a DaimlerChrysler subsidiary in southern Germany showed up at the opening ceremony to promote their engines for future yachts.

The generators come from Alaska Diesel Electric in Seattle. The interior lighting systems and the fabric for the upholstered chairs are also imported from the United States. So are the hinges for the shower doors. While the frosted glass is made locally, the hinges still have to be imported to make sure that the doors will open and close just right, said Olivia Liu, Kingship's interior decorator.

Kingship executives say they still have a competitive advantage because they are close to Chinese factories that increasingly dominate the world in the production of many materials, and the quality of local products is improving. They plan to start buying Chinese steel plates now that Corus and Multi Metaal have generated detailed computer data on the sizes and shapes needed.

Most important, Kingship has cheap labor that more than makes up for the extra shipping costs on imported parts.

Security guards, who make up about a tenth of the 200-person labor force, earn $120 a month, Mr. Yong said. Specialty skilled workers, like welders certified to international marine standards, can earn as much as $600 a month, a handsome salary in this country even if it is considerably less than a European marine welder makes in a week.

All workers live at the site in high-ceiling concrete barracks that, while spartan and crowded, are a big improvement over the huts nearby. Employees now sleep four to a room, though there are plans for eight to a room on bunk beds once the factory has a full order book and the work force has expanded to 500 people assembling seven vessels at a time.

Having the workers live on site helps when a yacht has to be refitted. They can work in shifts around the clock, day and night, to make sure that a vessel is ready in time for the summer or winter cruising season, Mr. Yong said.

"They want to earn more instead of idling around," he said, adding that the workers, mostly from elsewhere in China, did not have their families with them—a common practice in the country—and had little else to do. The company sent the workers away from the factory and barracks during the opening ceremony.

Western boat manufacturers say that the reliance here on imported parts, combined with a lack of local experience in assembling boats, means that they have little to fear. China's industry, they say, is too far behind to catch up quickly.

The quality of smaller boats already on the market from Chinese manufacturers "is still very poor," said Jeffrey Seah, general manager for China, Hong Kong and Taiwan at Mercury Marine, one of the world's largest boat-engine makers and a division of the Brunswick Corporation of Lake Forest, Ill.

"Chinese technology for boat building is 20 years behind," added Mr. Seah, whose company's China operation sells and distributes engines and operates a marina, hoping to interest more Chinese in leisure boating.

Lau Wai Keung, a marine engine specialist from China Engineers in Hong Kong who is helping Kingship install its Caterpillar engines, said that engines made in China were nowhere close to being competitive for use in yachts. A Chinese boat engine with the same horsepower as an American engine is 40 percent heavier and much bulkier, he said. That would mean a slower boat with a less roomy interior.

Foreign producers' confidence might seem misplaced, given China's growing export success with many other products, including high technology like notebook computers. Yet in the yacht market, Chinese manufacturers will not have the immediate feedback from local customers that their colleagues in other industries get for products with domestic sales.

A market has emerged for smaller vessels and marinas to hold them, and people who like the 40-footers might someday want the yachts being built by Kingship and Cheoy Lee. The China Jin Mao Group, a big property developer, has opened a boat club with a marina on the Huangpu River in Shanghai. The marina has five powerboats, up to 46 feet long and counted as commercial vessels, that can be chartered by the 1,800 club members, said Hu Yubo, the assistant general manager. Waiting lists to use the boats have the club planning to buy more.

The few, determined owners of the country's large powerboats sometimes fly in mechanics from Hong Kong and even Europe. And the mechanics must cope with a shortage of docks where yachts can be lifted out of the water.

Bart J. Kimman, a yacht broker with Simpson Marine, Asia's largest yacht brokerage company, says he discourages mainland Chinese tycoons from buying yachts unless they plan to keep them in Hong Kong, as a few have, even though regulations make it almost impossible to sail Hong Kong boats into mainland China waters. But Mr. Liang, after more than two decades as a big investor on the mainland, is not entirely sorry that he will have to stick to exports. He would rather not show his yachts to too many mainlanders.

"If you sell something well, someone will copy you," he said. "It happens right away."

15

Taking the World's Pulse: Global Health

Caroline Green

M edical research has taken huge strides in the past few decades. Thanks to the development of increasingly sophisticated drugs and a variety of technological breakthroughs, many people are enjoying a standard of health and wellbeing that would have been unimaginable a few generations ago.

But, overwhelmingly, it's the industrialised world that has benefited from these gains. In developing countries, infectious diseases, poverty, lack of clean water and inadequate healthcare continue to cause millions of preventable deaths every year.

And as globalisation shrinks boundaries and levels of human migration rise, health crises that would once have been restricted to a particular region are beginning to threaten the test of the world. The recent SARS outbreak demonstrated clearly how potentially lethal viruses can rapidly spread around the world.

In the first part of this month's dossier, Caroline Green examines how tuberculosis—a disease that doesn't hit the headlines with quite the same force as HIV or SARS—is quietly making a comeback. In part two, she assesses the extent to which the World Health Organization is achieving its objective of improving health for all, and in part three, she asks what needs to be done to improve child health in the developing world.

Geographical, March 2004, v76, i3, p34(9).

© 2004 Campion Interactive Publishing, Ltd.

DEFINITIONS

SARS: Severe acute respiratory syndrome, a viral respiratory illness that was first reported in Asia in February 2003 and quickly spread to more than two dozen countries in North and South America, Europe and Asia. DOTS: Directly observed treatment short-course, an initiative to combat tuberculosis that includes standardised diagnostics, national commitment and long-term drug programmes.

Antiretroviral drugs: a wide variety of different drugs that serve to inhibit HIV at different steps in its life cycle. Generally given as a cocktail in the hope that if the virus becomes resistant to one drug it will be knocked out by another, antiretrovirals can turn HIV/AIDS into a manageable chronic condition.

WHO: World Health Organization, the UN's special agency for health, established 7 April 1948. Its objective is to attain the highest possible level of health for people around the world.

THE RETURN OF A KILLER

Tuberculosis, the plague of the Victorians, has made a quiet, but significant comeback worldwide. But why? And what can be done to halt its spread?

Every second of every day, someone in the world is infected by the tuberculosis (TB) bacterium, and every year it kills two million people. The World Health Organization (WHO) estimates that between 2002 and 2020, one billion people will be newly infected, more than 150 million will fall ill and 36 million will die from the disease unless it is brought under effective control. Given that the disease was considered to be largely contained in the 1960s and '70s, these are worrying figures.

Rife during the 19th century—when it was known as consumption and claimed the lives of John Keats, Robert Louis Stevenson and seven members of the Bronte family—TB continued to be a major threat in the UK until the development of effective drug treatments after the Second World War. But elsewhere, in the absence of adequate healthcare systems, it remained endemic. According to Dr Matthew Gandy of University College London, the developed nations "took their eye off the ball" allowing the disease to spread once again, as air travel and migration increased.

In 1995, more people died from TB worldwide than in any other year. Shortly afterwards, the WHO declared the TB epidemic a global emergency. "TB respects no borders," says Dr Mario Raviglione, director of the WHO's Stop TB programme. "Either we control it globally or we have no way of controlling it. It has to be a global fight." The TB bacterium spreads through airborne droplets, in much the same way as the common cold. Each person with the active form of the disease is likely to infect 10–15 people every year. In about a third of the world's population it lies dormant, but it can be activated by anything that suppresses immunity, such as the stress of poverty, disease of poor living conditions.

Consequently, the most badly affected parts of the world are the poorest. "Two thirds of new cases are in Asia," says Raviglione, "and although the general trend is flat, there are two areas where it is rising—in sub-Saharan Africa and the 15 countries of the former Soviet Union." The latter cases involve a strain of TB that has become resistant to the main drugs used to treat it. It's so deadly that a Harvard University report referred to it as "ebola with wings". "This is vastly more expensive to treat than regular strains of TB," says Gandy. "If you don't have resources, it is effectively a death sentence."

As TB is an opportunistic infection that takes advantage of a weakened immune system, it also forms an unholy alliance with HIV/AIDS. In fact, it is the leading cause of death among people who are HIV-positive.

The biggest weapon against TB in the WHO's arsenal has been a strategy known as DOTS. This comprises five elements: a full government commitment to the fight against the disease; diagnosis based on a sputum smear test; a standard regimen of four drugs over six months; an effective system of drug supply; and an appropriate surveillance system to make sure patients take the full course of treatment. Raviglione says this is the only way that the disease can be properly controlled. "We are now really fighting on that front," he says. "We want to have the same standard of DOTS everywhere and need an intensification of countries' support."

Although DOTS has achieved some success, many believe the WHO must do more. One aid worker employed by a major NGO that focuses on health in the developing world, and who wishes to remain anonymous, says that the WHO has adopted "a Pollyanna approach" to DOTS. "It's better than any other random approach, but it's not good enough," she says. "The sputum test designed to pick up the disease was developed in 1882. It only picks up about SO per cent of cases." The drug therapies that are currently used in the treatment of TB are "sub-optimal", she says, making treatment regimens so long that many people don't bother to finish them. This, in turn, can lead to multi-drug resistance.

But there is hope for better treatments in the near future, although they've been a long time coming. The aid worker says that about 20 years ago there were off-the-shelf drugs that could cure TB, but they were never properly tested. Now that testing has been resumed, researchers are reporting cure rates of 97 per cent in just three months. Manageable short-term treatments such as these are vital, says the aid worker, especially in countries with limited resources. "The fact is that at some point we have to deal with the reality of TB."

TUBERCULOSIS IN THE UK

"TB has come back right into the heart of the developed world too," says Matthew Gandy. "The London Borough of Newham, for example, has higher rates of TB per head of population than India." As always, the disease proliferates in areas with poverty and overcrowding. In Brent, north London, the infection rate isn't very different to that found in parts of Thailand. It's recommended that children who are likely to be exposed to TB at a very young age are immunised, using the BCG vaccine, at birth; otherwise the vaccine is given to schoolchildren between the ages of ten and 14.

WHO: ON THE MEND?

To what extent has the World Health Organization lived up to its promise to deliver the highest possible level of health to the world?

The WHO's 1977 announcement signalled a major victory in its mission to improve the health of all on a local, national and international level. Smallpox, the 'ancient scourge' that at one stage threatened 60 per cent of the planet's population and killed every fourth victim, had been beaten following an intensive ten-year programme of immunisation. According to Graham Moon, professor of health geography at Portsmouth University, this remains the WHO's greatest achievement since it was set up in a spirit of post-war optimism in 1948.

But if the smallpox victory was the high-water mark of the organisation, the next two decades saw a decline to its lowest point. A report in the Medical Journal of Australia explains that this was a period in which it was "weakened...by zero growth in core budgets, diminished influence over the deployment of new sources of funding and with on-going challenges to its constitutional mandate". In the same article, Richard Horton, editor of the Lancet, accused the WHO of being "corrupt, bureaucratic, inefficient, unresponsive, overly medical and far too male".

In 1998, the ex-prime minister of Norway, Gro Harlem Brundtland, took over the post of director-general of the WHO, following the highly criticised ten-year office of Dr Hiroshi Nakajima. "The WHO was in a period of quite significant instability when Gro Harlem Brundtland took over," says Moon. "But it started to come back together quite substantially when she took over the reins. She pushed the organisation to look at some of the broader and wider issues surrounding global health and global health policy."

Brundtland focussed on four main areas within the WHO: building health communities on a national level; combating communicable and non-communicable diseases; promoting more transparent and accountable health systems; and improving the relationships between the WHO and other organisations. "There was a sense," says Moon, "that the organisation had become a little too 'medicalised' [rather than looking at these broader issues] but it does seem to be coming back now." In the Lancet, Richard Horton wrote, "She has successfully restored the WHO's international credibility, an achievement that seemed almost impossible five years ago."

So it was regarded as a disappointment by many when Brundtland announced in 2002 that she would not stand for re-election. In July 2003, her successor, Dr LEE Jong-wook pledged to focus on combating HIV/AIDS.

This renewed emphasis on a disease that the UN's AIDS agency, UNAIDS, has estimated will kill 68 million people prematurely in the next 20 years will centre around an ambitious plan to supply antiretroviral drugs to developing countries. By the end of 2005, it aims to have provided these potentially life-saving drugs to three million people, mainly in sub-Saharan Africa, which is nearly four times the total of all existing projects. The organisation plans to use its quick response to the SARS epidemic of 2003 as a model for dispatching medical teams to affected countries.

One of the criticisms of the pre-Brundtland WHO was that it placed too much emphasis on disease and ignored the wider issues surrounding health. "If you are going to get anywhere dealing with global health problems, particularly in developing countries," says Moon, "you need to engage very significantly with non-health intervention, particularly in relation to things such as clean water, sewage disposal and issues surrounding hunger and gender development." This broadening focus could be seen when the new HIV/AIDS programme was announced by the WHO in September 2003, as the organisation joined with the UN to condemn the West for spending billions on the 'War against terror' while failing to direct funds into HIV/AIDS-related programmes.

Whether the new WHO regime manages to tackle one of its on-going and biggest problems—that of over-bureaucratisation—remains to be seen. "It's an issue that has been addressed by recent directors-general," says Moon, "but it's a battle that isn't easily won. It's often seen that there are jobs for people who exist on a merry-go-round of international organisations."

The desire to deliver "the highest possible level of health" for all remains central to the mandate of the WHO, but 56 years since its birth, the new director-general must face up to challenges closer to home.

HIGHS AND LOWS OF THE WHO

The WHO has had some notable successes and failures.

Successes

- Eradication of smallpox
- Mother-and-child health programmes that encourage breastfeeding and immunise children against the biggest diseases of childhood—diptheria, tetanus, whooping cough, poliomyelitis and measles
- Influence on public-health systems, with emphasis on community health-care solutions
- Work with health systems in transition, such as those in the former Soviet states

Failures

- Inability to combat malaria (above), despite claims it would be eradicated
- Failure to combat cholera, diarrhoea and TB in poor countries
- Rising antibiotic resistance
- Continued rise in the number of HIV/AIDS infections

SUFFER THE CHILDREN

The West saw a vast improvement in child health in the 20th century. But in developing countries there is still a great deal of work to be done.

The past 30 years have seen some real improvements in the health of children worldwide. Overall, child mortality has been reduced, diarrhoea-related deaths have been halved and there has been a significant reduction in cases of polio, measles and neonatal tetanus, largely thanks to effective immunisation programmes. But these gains have been overwhelmingly made in industrialised countries, and the statistics covering children reveal the stark inequalities of global health.

According to Dr Nils Daulaire, president of the Global Health Council, there are two areas in which the divide between rich and poor countries is at its most obvious: the health and survival of children and the health and survival of mothers. Every year, more than ten million children under five die from preventable illnesses—that's 30,000 a day. More than 50,000 women die in pregnancy and childbirth, with deaths 100 times more likely in sub-Saharan Africa than in high-income OECD countries. "Illnesses such as diarrhoea, pneumonia and malaria remain the biggest killers of children in the developing world," says Regina Keith, health advisor to Save the Children. "Yet, with the right resources and policies, most of these diseases are preventable."

Of course, HIV/AIDS also lays a heavy burden on children, particularly in developing countries. The Global Health Council estimates that worldwide, nearly 600,000 children die from AIDS-related illnesses every year and that without antiretroviral treatment, 25–35 per cent of children born to HIV-positive mothers will contract the virus before, during or after birth. Today, there are also more than 14 million children who have lost one of both parents to AIDS.

Daulaire believes that the poor health of a nation's young has serious long-term economic implications. "Early deaths have a significant impact on countries," he says. "Research shows that for every child who dies, there are 20 who suffer and survive in a diminished state."

Dr Nicola Ansell, lecturer in human geography at Brunel University, is conducting research into these issues. She says that adolescent health can also have major implications for the future prospects of a population. "Adolescence has a bearing on later life," she says. "Malnutrition can cause permanent health problems, and it is estimated that 70 per cent of premature deaths among adults are attributed to behaviours initiated during adolescence."

Ansell has found some interesting patterns in the health of children and young people, even within the poorer countries. "Children within a household do not necessarily share equal chances of good health of even survival," she says. Worldwide, mortality rates among boys are higher in almost every country, and malnutrition rates are higher for boys everywhere apart from India and China. But she has also found that a country's poverty isn't in itself a guarantee that its child population will die young. In Sri Lanka, malnutrition rates are high, yet child mortality rates are low. This may be down to parents seeking outside help in instances where the major diseases of childhood are present.

Research has shown that maternal education and feeding practices play an enormous role in child health. According to the WHO, children who aren't breastfed are almost six times more likely to die within their first month than children who receive at least some breast milk. But although there are international controls on how formula milk is marketed in developing countries, it's still often promoted as a clean, healthy and modern food for babies. One study concluded that this turned mothers into "consumers of a commercial product they do not need and cannot afford and that contributes to the death of their infants".

The positive news, according to Professor Graham Moon of Portsmouth University, is that organisations such as the WHO have made a good deal of progress in promoting breastfeeding and other safe feeding practices. "It has played a major role by facilitating educationally based initiatives," he says.

But a major change in political will is needed to prevent a vast number of childhood deaths, say representatives of the WHO, Save the Children and the Global Health Council. "The present projected cost of basic healthcare is around US$30–40 [16 [pounds sterling]–22] per person in a developing country," says Regina Keith of Save the Children. "To achieve this, the Commission of Macroeconomics and Health has estimated that an extra US$27billion would need to be pledged by the G8 countries and more than US$30billion from developing countries themselves."

Executive director of UNICEF, Carol Bellamy has said, "The resources needed to reach every child and adolescent are well within the means of our wealthy worlds. Allocating a tiny fraction of those resources to [their needs] is an unparalleled investment in the health and security of our global community."

CHILD-HEALTH FACTS

- In high income countries, six out of every 1,000 children die before their fifth birthday. In the developing world, the rate can be as high as 120 per 1,000

- In 2003, 1.3 million children in developing countries died from diarrhoea
- Malnutrition contributes to 60 per cent of all deaths in childhood
- A child in a developing country is ten times more likely to die from a vaccine-preventable disease than one in a developed country
- Every year, eight million babies die within the first month of life
- Six hundred million children live on less than US$1 a day

16

Religion and Globalization

Ninian Smart

Once upon a time, in my young manhood, most people traveled overseas by ship. Few people—chiefly in relatively rich countries—traveled by plane. Now, virtually instantaneously, large numbers of people go from Osaka to Los Angeles, from Paris to Abidjan, from Montevideo to Colombo. The 1960s and 1970s saw the world explode with travel, connections, migrations, and exile. Those decades were also a time of religious contact on a new scale. By the 1980s and the 1990s first fax and then the Internet became popular communication vehicles. With the demise of the Soviet Union, a main bloc of closed communities crumbled. Global capitalism became vibrant and dominant. By the turn of the new century the religions of the world will have gotten to know one another quite well. What effect have all of these changes, which I will call globalization, had on the emotional lives of people and on the spirituality of the world?

Our new "smaller" world was created, in large part, by the two world wars and their subsequent inventions. The First World War not only spread conflict over a vast sector of the globe, but it also introduced many people to hitherto alien societies. The Second World War brought even more change. The jet plane was invented, and by the 1970s had given birth to jumbo jets—huge machines that conveyed large numbers of travelers over great distances. Many people had been displaced by the brutalities of the war, and many were still being dislodged in lesser conflicts: thus many poor people had access to other lands. Today Muslims, Hindus, Buddhists, Christians, and Jews live in countries far from those in which their religions originated.

ReVision, Fall 1999, v22, i2, p14.

© 1999 Heldref Publications.

In addition, during the colonial period some nationalities were systematically displaced. Africans were forced into the New World—Brazil, the Caribbean, America, and elsewhere; East Indians moved to South Africa, Fiji, and Guyana; Chinese emigrated to Singapore, Malaya, Indonesia, and the United States; and Japanese went to work in the Americas. All those migrations have brought increased pluralism and also susceptibility to prejudice.

Often immigrants set up places to gather and worship and simply kept to themselves. But over time that has begun to change. Second-generation children are taught the religious traditions, schools are set up, and immigrants read newspapers that report stories from home. All of that creates a sense of self-confidence, yet one's otherness is emphasized.

In many parts of the world diversity has been the norm. There have been Jews in Russia, Muslims in China, Protestants in France, Hindus in Sri Lanka, Copts in Egypt, Catholics in Vietnam, and so on—some for centuries, others for just a few years. Minorities have sometimes been persecuted, and in the time of the nation-state and globalization such oppressions have intensified. Often ethnic groups have been kept apart by distances; but now they must live face-to-face. While religions often preach tolerance and benevolence, they frequently emphasize otherness and hostility, which has contributed to global tensions.

Also, because tensions in one region are instantly known around the world, emigrants may become active and work to strengthen the resistance movements at home, which exacerbates the original antagonism. For example, at the present time, because there is a civil war between the Sinhalese and a sizable segment of the Tamils, a number of Tamils who live outside their country contribute to the war chest of Tamil resistance, which may intensify the struggle. So globalization brings people together, but it may also wrench them apart.

Religious communities face many issues in our tightly knit world. Since such a world creates the need for new approaches to education, partly so that less developed countries can be competitive with those that are rich in capital, technology, and military power, conflicts arise with tradition. Often a broader education is favored over older approaches. Now the glamour and persuasiveness of television and the Internet contribute significantly to such dilemmas. Often tensions revolve around questions of customs rather than education and for that reason are quite powerful. Should Jews wear yarmulkas in school? Should Muslim girls have veils? Ought Sikhs to wear turbans at work? Should restaurants owned by those who don't eat it for religious reasons serve pork to their customers?

The global world creates new dilemmas regarding scriptures and authorities. Those who treat divine revelation as absolute may try to impose their values on society. For instance, Islamic law may dominate Christian or Buddhist minorities who do not recognize it. In a plural world should all religious authorities be rejected? Yet atheism and agnosticism may equally be wrong. Whatever our values may be, they can be challenged by differing theories. Do all faiths point essentially to the one reality? Are there many paths to the same goal? Is only one fully correct? Maybe every faith has some truth, but one is truer than the others. By what criteria can one discover the truth or the best set of values? Are all faiths just bunkum? All those old questions are made more acute and pressing by the global order.

Such challenges to traditional religious thought can cause a conservative backlash. Often adherents of a religion become fundamentalist and highly reliant on a rather rigid interpretation of the revealed tradition, which tends to cause liberalism to wither and toleration to fade.

Colonialism helped to shape many of the patterns of contemporary religious life. Ideological and religious changes evolved in the period of struggle against imperialism. Although Japan, because of its farsighted modernization, joined the Western powers in the imperial enterprise (in China and Korea and in World War Two, for example), the military conquest of large sections of the world was overwhelmingly the undertaking of the Western powers, that is to say, Christian powers. So Catholicism, Protestantism, and Orthodoxy were spread into the countries of the Americas, Asia, Africa, and elsewhere. A plethora of new religions has arisen from the mingling of indigenous religions and Christianity.

As the cultures of Asia, the Middle East, and Africa began the march to independence—or freedom from the threat of the West, as in Japan and Thailand—they adopted various religious and ideological changes. Those changes were a necessary part of the transition from precolonialism to the modern world.

The residues of the last part of the nineteenth century to the first part of the twentieth century remain with us today and affect the process of globalization: for example the modern Hindu ideology, framed by Vivekananda, Gandhi, and Radhakrihman, behind Hindu nationalism; the modern sacred nationalism of Japan; the Maoism of China; the new Theravada of South East Asia; the Islamic modernism and secular socialism of the Arab world; and the negritude of Africa. All of those forces have faded and have been partially replaced in the second part of the twentieth century. Hinduism has been effective in preserving traditions. Japan's modernization has been successful, even though it was interrupted by World War Two. China's Maoism, though disastrous to traditional values, has produced a new independence. South East Asia has been prey to warfare and radical ideologies. A fundamentalist Islam has begun to replace Arab nationalism. Independent churches have been a vital force in subSaharan Africa, driven however by old borders and the fragmentation of languages and societies. The collapse of the Soviet union leaves many traces of the old order there.

With the advent of space travel the Earth is now seen in all its beauty and environmental fragility, which gives new symbolic dimension to globalization. Sometimes called Gaia, it is a living entity that sustains us all: We cannot think of the human race without having a feeling for our world as a whole and humanity as one.

Though our world is increasingly perceived of as a shared whole with its people more and more intertwined in terms of race, nationality, and religion, it still remains carved up into sovereign states. That fact generates a strong sense of nationalism, which affects religions. There is a tendency to think of states as essentially Christian, Islamic, Buddhist, and so on. Yet at the same time religions usually claim to have a universal message. I will address that apparent contradiction later in this article.

Nationalism, though it has ritual, ethics, and mythology, is devoid of doctrines; for this reason it often arms itself with a religion or an ideology. Thus Polish nationalism allies itself with Catholicism, Vietnamese with Marxism, Sinhala with Buddhism, Pakistani with Islam, and so on.

Conversations about religion and globalization must consider the importance of modern science. Physics, biology, and the rest of the "hard" sciences are in principle unified. Whereas nationality may be important in religion, history, or literature, science ignores it. That there has to be global astronomy or physics suggests something about the nature of truth.

The single truth of science contrasts with the multiple truths of religion and of humanity's values, which are complex and detailed. What is the future of science? Will it manage to piece together human consciousness? Will it delineate, through further study of the brain, the nature of religious experience?

Atheism is a vital intellectual force around the globe. It was a feature of Marxism, which was the ideology of the Soviet empire, much of Eastern Europe and Cuba, and parts of Africa. In a different form, atheism controlled China. In the Western world it had less influence. In France and Italy it had a grip on powerful political parties. In the United States it is a common view held by intellectuals. Atheism is an important value that must be taken seriously. At the same time, Orthodoxy and other religious movements have revived in the former Soviet countries.

At the present time, the world is in the grip of a kind of "free market" capitalism, which can be praised for its polycentrism and its help to wavering democracy. It contains notable inconsistencies, relevant to human values and therefore to religion. States naturally fund armies, military enterprises, and hardware, which is not considered socialism, though it has a similar effect. It is relatively easy in the Western world to get funds for armies, prisons, and other primitive enterprises. But is it easy to get money for welfare? Often those values are contrary to the teachings of the world's religions, yet the attitude of religions is often highly ambiguous.

Another element of globalization, which results in part from the spread of education, is the strong nisus toward individualism. Evident in New Age thinking, it can also be seen in the various dimensions of religion. Initially that will make scriptures seem more important: The Bible, the Qur'an, the Upanishads, and so forth might have a powerful effect on individuals. A more literal adherence to the revelation or authority will likely result or the opposite more flexible and tolerant loyalty to the tradition may result. That rather intense division between the fundamentalist and liberal varieties of religion has become a feature of our globalized world.

All of the features of globalization that I have mentioned have an effect on the various aspects of religion—its doctrinal or philosophical aspects, its ethical and legal meaning, its experiential and emotional side, its organizational or social outreach activities, its ritual and practical expression, and its mythic and narrative dimension.

For example, regarding religious and philosophical doctrine, there are always some modifications to cosmology due to advances and changes in science; and these have to be incorporated by religions that have a traditional view of the scale of the universe (notably the three theistic religions stemming from the Hebrew Bible). Moreover, the issue of life in this (possibly teaming) universe raises questions about the literal uniqueness of Christ. Again, biology suggests that the doctrine of karma would have to be reshaped. The practical consequences of, for example, nuclear proliferation and modern methods of birth control and surgery present ethical dilemmas for many traditional values. Other ethical challenges are made more acute by the widening gap between rich and poor spawned by modern capitalism.

The experiential factor is affected in many ways. For example, the methods of yoga and Eastern religion are enhanced by modern migrations and communications. Shamans have their contemporary counterparts in spiritual leaders with numerous and various visions.

Religious organizations often imitate one another. Frequently the methods of Christian missionaries are taken over by other religions. The smaller religions have begun to make alliances and to coalesce (consider African religions and Native American religions). Diasporas are becoming united through new ways of communicating and by exchanging specialist personnel (such as priests, monks, and mullahs). Because of the pluralism of so many societies, education, factors such as social mobility, and movements from the countryside to urban sprawls, there is a decline in authority and traditional customs.

At the same time the mythic or narrative dimensions of religion are changing. In the early 1960s I first heard mention of historical dates in regard to Rama and Krishna, for instance, as if they were actual historical individuals. That in part is an attempt to give literal truth to what had been symbolic. Today people are less inclined to believe myths, like that of Adam and Eve; they interpret the stories more abstractly. The great attraction of Marxism, I believe, was that it replaced myth with abstract narratives. Some contemporary Christian theology has pioneered ways to "demythologize" the New Testament. As the world grows smaller and more competitive those tendencies have intensified.

At the organizational level, we might also take note of an increasing individualism. People are no longer afraid of excommunication, and as a result they feel free to be much more eclectic in their beliefs. One of the manifestations of that freer spirit is New Age religion (to its detractors, it is shockingly zany in its superstitions; but to its supports it exhibits a great tolerance).

Most important, how is the ritual dimension of religion affected by the new world order? Already communications have helped to transform pilgrimages, an important ritual activity in many religions. Practically all Muslims have swift access to the hajj and to Mecca, which before modern air travel was an immense undertaking for many. The Pope, the object of much ritual attention, travels around the world by jet, becoming accessible to millions who would never be able to travel to Rome. Fifty years ago going to church was a serious activity; now it is briefer and more entertaining. Television religion in which viewers can participate in the reenactment of the Hindu epics, the singing of hymns, the enactment of the feasts of the Buddha, and so on, has developed. Globalization has evolved against the background of the new hope given the religions since the time of colonialism.

In Europe Christianity is remarkably weak, especially in Britain, France, and Scandinavia. Even in Catholic countries, such as Italy, it is now a good deal less prevalent than it was. Agnosticism is vital through most of Europe. However, Christianity has undergone a revival in the former Soviet sphere, notably Orthodoxy in Russia and Romania, and Catholicism in Poland.

North America, like Europe, has a large immigrant population. In Europe, Turks, Pakistanis, Africans, Indians, and so on, represent large minorities; in North America, apart from traditional minorities, such as the Jews and blacks, there are large numbers of immigrants from around the world. But both America and Canada are largely Protestant and Catholic, though they have a substantial proportion of people who are not attached to any religious tradition or are moving into Buddhism and other faiths originating in other cultures. Native American peoples have a vital religious culture. In Central and South America, especially from Mexico down to Paraguay, where the indigenous population is significant, the Catholic Church holds sway, though in the last forty years Protestant forms have gained increasing influence. The Caribbean is a vibrant society that includes Christians, Hindus, practitioners of African-based religions, and so forth. Caribbean culture has had a strong influence in North America and has also left its mark on Britain.

Maoris, Aboriginals, Native Americans, and so on live as minorities in predominantly Western cultures. The same is true on many continents: the Sami in Scandinavia; shaman-oriented smaller societies in Siberia; the Hmong and Toraja in South East Asia; tribal peoples in India, etc. Perhaps the day will come when those minorities will form mutual alliances in order to gain strength.

Because modern developments in religion, especially those influenced by the colonial period and the world wars have had an important effect on the way the religions manifest, I want to review the religious trends as I understand them. By the latter half of the nineteenth century it was obvious, or beginning to be obvious, to the peoples of Asia that they had to do something about the Europeans (and then later the Americans). Whereas northern Asia was lightly inhabited, the south—East Asia, China, South East Asia and South Asia—was the site of several major civilizations.

In India (including what is now Pakistan and Bangladesh) the British conquest brought political unification, a more or less unified administration, and a railway system. The educational change was profound. In some ways, traditions were threatened, and the greater scale of unity underlined the grave differences between the Muslims and Hindus in particular. But the renewal of Sanskrit scholarship and the challenges and opportunity of the new learning created a new chance for Hinduism to express itself. The thinking of Vivekanada, who inspired Gandhi, and other notions helped to make a relatively eirenic nationalism possible. Its idea that all religions point to the same truth reflected something in the Hindu tradition and meant also that Muslims, Jains, Christians, Zoroastrians, and others could join together to work for India. But also it was inclusive, so that India's agglutinative genius was expressed. India's tolerant constitution was able to let ancient and modern, spiritual and material, custom and education live together. It happened too that the independence movement could work with the British; and although there was grievous bloodshed between Hindus and Muslims, that was the result of popular distrust, not a policy of the emerging new ruling class. But with time, the continuing poverty of India's growing underclass (largely caused by India's failure to curb its population growth) helped to give an impetus to a new Hindu lobby. That may exacerbate the relations between Muslims and Hindus and between Pakistan and India. But in general India has managed to build on its tradition, to modernize, and to hold the differing values together.

The history of China during this century has been less fortunate. The collapse of the old China, with its examination system, was brought about chiefly by the erosion of the empire resulting from the incursion of the Western powers and Japan. Also the enormous Taiping Rebellion during the middle of the nineteenth century had a sapping effect. There was hardly a relevant middle class (in the Western sense); the ambitious democracy of Sun Yat-sen was not destined to last; and the military dictatorship had insufficient discipline to win the civil war. As it was, Mao expressed a form of Marxism adapted to the Chinese condition. But the fact that Marxism was the enemy of colonialism (as was thought) and capitalism did not mean that it was good for China. In the Mao years, the major traditions of China (Confucianism, Taoism, and Buddhism, together with Islam and Christianity) were virtually destroyed. Since the late 1970s there has been some degree of restoration. Admittedly a kind of capitalism was encouraged, with some success. But China remains somewhat confused. If the name of the game is to modernize and yet retain as much of your tradition as possible, China has not been successful.

Korea was ready to emerge into the modern era, when it was suddenly conquered by Japan. Mainly Confucian and Buddhist in its heritage, it was now subject to Christian, mainly Protestant, missionaries. Except for the Philippines, which was subject to a Catholic colonizing power and did not have a basis in Chinese values, Korea is the most Christian country in Asia. After World War Two it experienced the trauma of being divided into two countries. Though it has revived economically, there is a question as to how far Korea can build on its Neoconfucian and Buddhist ideals. That uneasy compromise between the tradition and modernity is a challenge for Korea's future.

Japan was far-sighted during the Meiji restoration. It reworked its head of
state, reeducated itself in Western ways, adopted a new constitution, invented
modern industry, and built a fleet and an army. Amazingly, within less than
forty years it had defeated the Russians at Tsushima. It also had devised a new
Shinto able to act as a general focus of loyalty for the population. But by World
War Two Japan had become overconfident. But despite its eventual, crushing
defeat, Japan was able to build a renewed economy. The new society seems to
be 50 percent traditional and 50 percent Western with a future that is hard to
predict.

South East Asia has for a time succumbed to differing forms of Marxism,
though the Khmer Rouge is more what I would call post–Buddhist. Their
ideology called for an ideal society, which was not capitalist, hence the killing
fields: Anyone with Western (or even Buddhist) education had to be eliminated. On the other hand, Vietnam was more traditionally Marxist. Ideology
in general seems to be dying. Thailand hopes for a more or less liberal future.
Burma aims for a collective nirvana, isolated from the world. The same sort of
ideal was found among the original JVP in Sri Lanka. It is as if when Buddhist
countries go mad, they do so in similar ways. Where Buddhism reigns unfettered, as in Thailand and Sri Lanka, it is relatively liberal and outward-looking
in its doctrines.

In Indonesia, Malaysia, and elsewhere where Islam holds sway in Southeast
Asia, it is relatively liberal. Indonesia holds a version of the Hindu doctrine:
All religions search for God. That is in part a tribute to the diversity of the
Indonesian islands. But is Indonesia a unity? The rigidity of the regime, even
after Suharto, shows how fissiparous the islands are. By an irony, the unity of
Indonesia is simply a result of Dutch conquest. Though the configuration of
the modern world is based on nations and empires, those lines between them
may not be valid ones. But since Indonesian Islam is built on the ideology of
Pancasila (five fundamental principles), it is relatively liberal.

As China reaches into Central Asia, boundaries become fuzzy. Western
China, occupied by Muslims and by the Tibetans, is not Han, though Hans
have of course settled there in recent times. Generally speaking, minority
peoples in China as elsewhere, want independence, a desire that is often
reinforced by religion. Tibetans are a different ethnic group and are more
strongly Buddhists. It is tempting for Chinese, as the dominant ethnic group,
to continue to assert their power over those subject people. The world needs
to decide whether or not to intervene to liberate the Tibetan people.

Over three hundred years ago the Russians conquered Siberia, a sparsely
populated area. Russia was in many ways outside the European mainstream.
After being crippled by World War I, Russia executed communist revolution.
The new system was built on hope, but it involved tyranny too. Does that
largely collapsed ideology have possibilities for renewal? In the rest of Europe,
communism merged with social democracy, but Russia remains one of the
world's areas of instability. In a sense the communism of the twentieth century
was a positive response to a semicolonial condition with positive features such

as strong scientific education, but it turned out to have destructive and woe-fully oppressive qualities (as smaller societies in Siberia would attest). Despite the revival of religion in the former Soviet Union, a large atheistic minority exists as a direct consequence of the regime.

Central Asia and the Caucasus were also dominated by communism, but partly because the religion of Sufism was less susceptible to state control, that area survived the Soviet period. Throughout the region there is a significant minority of Russians, which has led to some cultural complications.

The Middle East, from Iran through the Arab States in North Africa, had a curious colonial history. The Arab lands were part of the Ottoman Empire, in some respects premodern in outlook. That empire was overthrown after World War I, but to the west, French and Italian colonialism, and Egypt, longest under Western domination, persisted under British rule. Syria, Lebanon, Jordan, Iraq, and the smaller states were under French and British colonial rule after the Ottoman Empire collapsed. Saudi Arabia was under the Wahhabi (quasi-fundamentalist Islamist) royal family. While Egypt emerged from colonial rule after World War II as a relatively liberal state, with an im-portant middle class, most of the Arab nations fell under military dictatorship, with one or two royal houses. On the whole the ideology had a pan-Arab motif, Islamist forces constitute a minority force but have not gained control. But in Iran, beyond the Arab world, that Islamic ideology gained control in 1979 under the leadership of the Ayatollah Khomeini. Generally, the Arab re-sponse to the West has been to adopt a degree of modernism not always intel-ligibly related to the Islamic tradition.

Africa, despite the grip of classical African religions on their societies, has undergone considerable penetration both by Islam and both Catholic (espe-cially in Francophone countries) and Protestant missions. Nevertheless, while classical African religions have persisted, by far the largest response is in so-called independent churches, where Christian and indigenous ideas and prac-tices have blended. The weakness of the independent churches has been a lack of doctrinal sophistication, but no doubt that will be remedied. By giving genuine African leadership (always suspect in the mainstream traditions) and by incorporating African spirituality and healing practices, it may be that they have a role to play in the new global culture.

All those postcolonial forces have come together in the new globalist world. As recent history in so many countries has indicated, there remain many bitter conflicts, often of a religious nature (Cyprus, Israel, India-Pakistan, Sri Lanka, Indonesia, Myanmar, and elsewhere). But at the same time in democratic countries and elsewhere a genuine interplay between religions is taking place, which suggests many questions.

Will the globe develop its own single narrative—a history of the heroes of all nations? Will we perhaps as a human race gain a sense of harmony through a genuinely shared past? The question remains whether we will eventually come together in a common ideology.

InfoMarks: Make Your Mark

What Is an InfoMark?

It's a single-click return ticket to any page, any result, any search from InfoTrac College Edition.

An InfoMark is a stable URL, linked to InfoTrac College Edition articles that you have selected. InfoMarks can be used like any other URL, but they're better because they're stable—they don't change. Using an InfoMark is like performing the search again whenever you follow the link—whether the result is a single article or a list of articles.

How Do InfoMarks Work?

If you can "copy and paste," you can use InfoMarks.

When you see the InfoMark icon on a result page, its URL can be copied and pasted into your electronic document—Web page, word processing document, or email. Once InfoMarks are incorporated into a document, the results are persistent (the URLs will not change) and are dynamic.

Even though the saved search is used at different times by different users, an InfoMark always functions like a brand new search. Each time a saved search is executed, it accesses the latest updated information. That means subsequent InfoMark searches might yield additional or more up-to-date information than the original search with less time and effort.

Capabilities

InfoMarks are the perfect technology tool for creating:

- Virtual online readers
- Current awareness topic sites—links to periodical or newspaper sources
- Online/distance learning courses
- Bibliographies, reference lists
- Electronic journals and periodical directories
- Student assignments
- Hot topics

Advantages

- Select from over 15 million articles from more than 5,000 journals and periodicals
- Update article and search lists easily
- Articles are always full text and include bibliographic information
- All articles can be viewed online, printed, or emailed
- Professors and students save time
- Anyone with access to InfoTrac College Edition can use it
- No other online library database offers this functionality
- FREE!

How to Use InfoMarks

There are three ways to utilize InfoMarks—in HTML documents, Word documents, and email

HTML Document

1. Open a new document in your HTML editor (Netscape Composer or FrontPage Express).
2. Open a new browser window and conduct your search in InfoTrac College Edition.
3. Highlight the URL of the results page or article that you would like to InfoMark.
4. Right click the URL and click Copy. Now, switch back to your HTML document.
5. In your document, type in text that describes the InfoMarked item.
6. Highlight the text and click on Insert, then on Link in the upper bar menu.
7. Click in the link box, then press the "Ctrl" and "V" keys simultaneously and click OK. This will paste the URL in the box.
8. Save your document.

Word Document

1. Open a new Word document.
2. Open a new browser window and conduct your search in InfoTrac College Edition.
3. Check items you want to add to your Marked List.
4. Click on Mark List on the right menu bar.
5. Highlight the URL, right click on it, and click Copy. Now, switch back to your Word document.
6. In your document, type in text that describes the InfoMarked item.
7. Highlight the text. Go to the upper bar menu and click on Insert, then on Hyperlink.

8. Click in the hyperlink box, then press the "Ctrl" and "V" keys simultaneously and click OK. This will paste the URL in the box.
9. Save your document.

Email

1. Open a new email window.
2. Open a new browser window and conduct your search in InfoTrac College Edition.
3. Highlight the URL of the results page or article that you would like to InfoMark.
4. Right click the URL and click Copy. Now, switch back to your email window.
5. In the email window, press the "Ctrl" and "V" keys simultaneously. This will paste the URL into your email.
6. Send the email to the recipient. By clicking on the URL, he or she will be able to view the InfoMark.